AF396624

COVER: photo DR

ACKNOWLEDGEMENTS: We would like to give our warmest thanks to the Directors of our academic institutions for their precious support, Pierre-Jean Galdin, Christian Dautel, Rozenn Le Merrer, Daniel Siret, and Thomas Leduc, as well as our colleagues from the AAU-CRENEAU (UMr 1563 CNRS/ENSAG/ECN), the Nantes Saint-Nazaire School of Art, and the Graduate School of the Nantes National Architecture School, for their generous assistance.

We would like to extend our thanks to Karine Bellosta, Marine Bouquet, Maï Tran, Véronique Dom, Leïla Zerrouki, Alice Albert, Elise Bouvry, as well as to Capucine Lageat and Antoine Perroteau, and of course to all the other people who have contributed to this project.

WITH THE SUPPORT OF

MINISTÈRE DE LA CULTURE
AAU CRENAU
BEAUX-ARTS NANTES SAINT-NAZAIRE
ENSA NANTES

Thinking from the Border, a project that brings together research professors from the CRENAU (Nantes Urban Architecture Research Center) at the Nantes Graduate School of Architecture, and from the Nantes Saint-Nazaire School of Art.

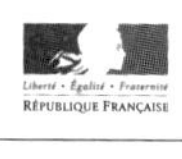
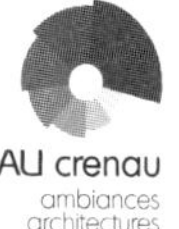
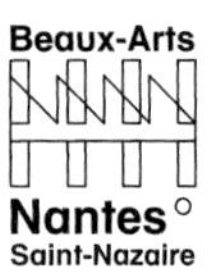
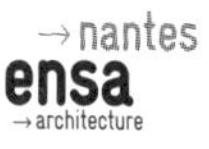

THINKING FROM THE BORDER

METHODOLOGICAL AND EPISTEMOLOGICAL EXPERIMENTATIONS
BETWEEN THE ARTS AND THE HUMAN SCIENCES

ANNE BOSSÉ

CHRISTIANE CARLUT

EMMANUELLE CHÉREL

AMÉLIE NICOLAS

ELISABETH PASQUIER

VÉRONIQUE TERRIER HERMANN

translated from French by
CHARLES LA VIA

see our complete catalogue on: www.disvoir.com

series ART VISUAL ESSAYS edited by
DANIELE RIVIERE

in the same series "visual arts/ essay"

BRITISH BLACK ART
DEBATES ON WESTERN ART HISTORY
Sophie Orlando

MNEMOSYNE
A HISTORY OF THE ARTS OF MEMORY FROM ANTIQUITY TO CONTEMPORARY MULTIMEDIA CREATION
François Boutonnet

THE IMAGE-MATTER
EMERGING MATERIALS AND IMAGINARY METAMORPHOSIS
Dominique Peysson

THE MUTANT FLESH
FABRICATION OF A POSTHUMAN
Denis Baron

NARRATIVITY: HOW VISUAL ARTS, CINEMA AND LITERATURE ARE TELLING THE WORLD TODAY
René Audet, Claude Romano, Laurence Dreyfus, Carl Therrien, Hugues Marchal

BLACK IS A COLOR: A HISTORY OF AFRICAN AMERICAN ART
Elvan Zabunyan

KEEP THIS SEX OUT OF MY SIGHT
Elvan Zabunyan, Chrystel Besse, Arlette Fontan, Françoise Gaillard, Marie-Joseph Bertini

CONTEMPORARY PRACTICES: ART AS EXPERIENCE
Paul Ardenne, Pascal Beausse, Laurent Goumarre

TECHNO: AN ARTISTIC AND POLITICAL LABORATORY OF THE PRESENT
Michel Gaillot, Jean-Luc Nancy, Michel Maffesoli

SOUND AND THE VISUAL ARTS
Jean-Yves Bosseur

IN FAVOUR OF TODAY'S ART
François Dagognet

CONTENTS

ABOUT THE AUTHORS

Anne Bossé is an architect and geographer. She teaches at the *Ecole nationale supérieure d'architecture de Paris Malaquais*, and is a member of the urban architecture research team at the French National Center for Scientific Research (CRENAU, CNRS). Her research on public spaces focuses on their material and political dimensions, and on the hybridization linking the conditions of immigrants and material culture. She has also recently studied the processes of negotiation in the construction of mosques in western France, and the fabrication of users in the urban management of proximity.

Christiane Carlut is a filmmaker http://christiane-carlut.fr/christiane-carlut/ and a professor at the Nantes Saint-Nazaire School of Art. She has organized various artistic events, including the Copyright/Copywrong colloquium, and given talks and written texts on artistic freedom of appropriation (Copyleft). She is also the president of an association that defends the rights of foreigners. Her work in progress is a trilogy of movies, *La figure noire du figurant,* and an alternative reality multimedia platform on the Paris Commune, *Le luxe Communal,* with assistance from the *Friends of the Commune.*

Emmanuelle Chérel, is a Professor of Art History and a member of the urban architecture research team at the French National Center for Scientific Research (CRENAU, CNRS). Her research focuses on the political dimensions of art and draws on theoretical interdisciplinary tools and approaches to resituate an artistic proposition within the context in which it appeared, so it can be observed as an act accomplished within a historical reality. Her current work focuses on the postcolonial in the field of art today. She teaches at the Nantes Saint-Nazaire School of Art, where she directs a research project on archipelagic thinking. Some of her numerous articles have been published in *Archives de la critique d'art, Multitudes, Black Camera, Journal des laboratoires d'Aubervilliers, l'art même*, and *May*, as well as a study *The Nantes Memorial for the Abolition of Slavery – Issues and Controversies*. She also co-edited with Fabienne Dumont *Art History Under the Radar: Art and Postcoloniality in France.*

Amélie Nicolas has a Ph.D. in sociology. She is a professor at the *Ecole nationale supérieure d'architecture de Paris Malaquais*, and a researcher on the urban architecture team at the French National Center for Scientific Research (CRENAU, CNRS). Her specific research focuses on government and urban policies, memory-based conflicts in the framework of urban projects, and more generally on contexts of urban decline. She develops her research mainly within the framework of an ethnographic methodology.

Elisabeth Pasquier is a Professor of Sociology who conducts research for the urban architecture research team at the French National Center for Scientific Research (CRENAU, CNRS). Her research focuses on "spatialized" popular cultures and how they are recomposed in connection with migratory and transnational processes. It is related to theories of the "arts of doing," which intersect spatial practices and language use. She also experiments with enunciative forms linked to social issues and reassesses the place and the meaning of research in society.

Véronique Terrier Hermann, is a contemporary art historian whose research focuses on Images and Visual Culture. She works as a curator, and research professor at the Nantes Saint-Nazaire School of Art, and is also in charge of the Research and Creation Support Program of the Photo Institute in Lille. Her research and work focus more specifically on how contemporary art interplays with cinema and documentary.

THINKING FROM THE BORDER *

*I*nitiated by a multidisciplinary group that brings together sociologists, art historians, and artists, the research project and book *Thinking from the Border* borrows its title from the philosopher Sandro Mezzadra.[1]

Its title insists on a common concern: How can one work from the border? A complex question that stems from the significant transformations of the contemporary world. The border was first considered as a methodological issue, a chance to devote our attention and commit ourselves to a collective undertaking that would produce inquiries, writing, and artworks within a wide range of research areas. Based on these individually imagined and completed research projects, we were able to bring together our ideas around common issues, around the paradoxical processes of globalization, as well as the transformations of our theoretical tools and conditions as researchers. We examined in particular transnational effects, the circulation and migration of ideas, references, and bodies, the contemporaneousness of several worlds, the temporal co-presence of different epistemologies, as well as the processes through which the Other is invented. Each of these reflections on the transformations linked to globalization is rooted in the following contemporary epistemological questions: From what position do we speak? What is our situation with respect to our fields of study? How do we redefine our approaches and theoretical tools? What dialogues do we maintain with the tools of intellectuals from different countries of the South? The border conceived as subject and method is the interdisciplinary, epistemic frame that has enabled us to study

* Project that brings together research professors from the CRENAU (Nantes Urban Architecture Research Center) at the Nantes Graduate School of Architecture, and from the Nantes Saint-Nazaire School of Art.
[1] Sandro Mezzadra, Brett Neilson, *Border as Method, or The Multiplication of Labor*, London, Durham, Duke University Press, 2013.

certain practices and methodological issues, while also redefining paradigms and concepts.

This collective research program is being continued,[2] and it extends our common interests[3] in areas of experimental studies that blur the boundaries between disciplines, creating interdisciplinary projects between the arts and the human sciences, and especially so that the methodologies of the human sciences and artistic practices are more tightly interwoven.

What Constitutes a Border?

The question of the border has been widely studied in recent years, because this issue is omnipresent in the media as well as in our daily lives. The appearance of new state borders, border tensions, and geopolitical events are directly linked to the exploding interest in this subject.[4]

The border can be defined as a political construct that can take on various concrete forms such as a mountain, a river, or a wall. It is also considered to be dynamic, evolving, and historicized, and more or less impenetrable and stable. For those who observe it, and in general, the border is both a line (that separates and creates discontinuity) and a zone of contact (that enables all kinds of symbolic, material, peaceful, and violent exchanges). Originating from concerns that are essentially political and strategic, and linked in particular to

[2] The question of the (intercultural) border had already been studied by the LAUA (Language, Urban Actions, Alterities Laboratory—now the CRENAU); in particular, how it is embodied in urban and public spaces in Nantes (a study on Islam in Nantes, and one on the monument that commemorates the abolition of slavery). Meanwhile, the Nantes School of Art had undertaken a certain number of projects including artist residencies and research projects within the scope of issues related to art and globalization.

[3] The research undertaken within the *Thinking from the Border* project was continued for three years in two seminars. In 2014, *Le peuple qui manque* with talks by the geographer Valérie Gelezeau, the artist Augustin Gimmel, the geographer Anne-Laure Amilhat Szary, the political scientist Françoise Vergès, critics, and curators. In 2015, *Questions historiographiques* with talks by the historian Philippe Artières, the artist Vincent Meessen, and the art historian Vanessa Théodoropoulou. In addition, there was a cycle of films coordinated by Véronique Terrier Hermann with the association Contrechamp at the Cinématographe movie theater. In March 2018, this research took on the form of public workshops and exhibitions at the Nantes Saint-Nazaire Fine Arts School.

[4] See https://ifd.hypotheses.org/bibliographie-sur-les-frontieres

the strengthening of nation states (of how they control the enemy within, such as regional minorities, and the conquest of foreign territories), border studies became a scientific discipline in the nineteenth century,[5] before undergoing a profound change: formerly a line, the border has become a zone; once physical, it is now cultural.[6]

These renewed approaches to borders and borderlands drew fruitfully upon research from a wide range of disciplines. In the present day, geographical, national and political boundaries are continuously questioned and transgressed, subjected to accelerated geographic mobility, movements of people (for tourism, migration, and professional mobility), financial flows, and trade, as well as virtual mobility via internet, and the movement of images and information. All of these phenomena stem from globalization, urban development, and the digital transformation of societies. However, the elimination of some borders does not occur without the appearance of new boundaries and separations in the form of forced sedentariness, communities that isolate themselves from society, nationalists, and ethnic groups.[7]

Other discontinuities are emerging. Borders are being redeployed in response to effects from various force fields, such as the big boom of religion, the dominant economic logics, political systems, armed conflicts, cross-cultural intersections, topography, and ecological issues. They delineate, frame, and include as much as they exclude with their limits, lawless areas, and potential reserves. Successively denied, reaffirmed, redrawn by the continuous shifts in linguistic, cultural, and political boundaries, they are constantly being modified[8] and bear witness to the incompletability of the world and its transformations.

[5] Michel Foucher, *Le retour des frontières*, (Paris CNRS, 2016).

[6] Arjun Appadurai, *Modernity at Large. Cultural Dimensions of Globalization,* (Minneapolis: University of Minnesota Press, 1996).

[7] 14,700 kilometers of new borders have been created in Europe since 1990, not to mention those in Asia or on the edges of Russia. The creation of new borders, and the evolution of the very concept of border, help us understand that they are a social product that has been progressively built by societies to divide the world.

[8] The human border has its own limits, whereas certain non-humans ignore borders, as we can see in the migrations of plant species in response to global warming.

In his article *"What is a Border*?", the philosopher Etienne Balibar writes: "*The idea of a simple definition of what constitutes a 'border' is by definition absurd: for drawing a border means in fact defining a territory, delineating one, and in this act establishing or conferring upon it its identity. Yet inversely, defining and identifying in general is nothing more than drawing a border, setting boundaries (in Greek, horos; in Latin finis or terminus; in German Grenze; in English border). The theorist who wants to define the concept of 'border' is in a Catch-22 situation, because the very representation of the border is the condition for any definition of it.*[9] Balibar attempts nonetheless to demarcate the notion through four characteristics: *overdetermination, polysemy, heterogeneity,* and *ubiquity*. In other words, when facing the multiplicity of border situations and experiences, we must avoid simplistic and problematic reductions. A border materializes at places of active tensions between antagonistic logics, and often beyond official territorial demarcations. It is not necessarily where we expect it to be. The accurate appraisal of the place of borders in our societies would require us to take account of many considerations other than the voluntary limitation of (not) crossing an imaginary line drawn on the ground. The anthropologist James Clifford has, for example, examined a series of places in which culture is *in transition*—places he calls *"borderlands."*[10]

He finds colliding and changing cultures as readily in art museums as in Mayan ruins, the New York subway, and urban spaces. Numerous studies in human and political sciences have taken up these questions in recent years. A specific field of studies (*Border Studies*[11]) has also come

[9] Etienne Balibar, "Qu'est-ce qu'une frontière?", in Marie-Claire Caloz-Tschopp, Axel Clevenot (editors), *Asile, violence, exclusion en Europe: histoire, analyse, prospective,* (Geneva: University of Geneva, 1994), 335-343. All translations of citations are by Charles A. La Via, unless otherwise indicated.
[10] James Clifford, *Routes: Travel and Translation in the Late Twentieth Century,* (Cambridge, Harvard University Press, 1997).
[11] Border Studies: Remapping the Humanities." Border Studies: A website exhibit produced by the Texas Humanities Resource Center.

into existence. The approaches of *Postcolonial Studies,*[12] which aim to deconstruct modern divisions and how they were established— borders created by colonization and conceptual borders stemming from old ontological maps (human/non-human) and gender-based boundaries (men/women)—, have also lead to a reconsideration of our relationship to space and time, that is, to complex contemporary temporalities and spatialities.

Thus, some of the projects carried out in the framework of *Thinking from the Border* reflect on the articulations between different scales and territories, on visible and invisible borders as institutions and sets of social relations, on the circumstances, tensions, and conflicts they translate and generate, on the multiple dynamics and negotiations, on the evolution of the concepts of citizenship and sovereignty. In their article "Following the Dead in their Migrations" Anne Bossé and Elisabeth Pasquier focus on a subject that has received little attention in the social sciences: how the bodies of French people of foreign descent are repatriated to their homelands. These corpses themselves defined the investigative process implemented: on the one hand, observing the situations in which these corpses circulate and interact with the living; on the other, the "conveyors" (close friends or relatives who accompany the body) were interviewed to give life to the narratives of these repatriations. The will to study repatriations as transnational practices highlights the ways in which the lives of people who have immigrated (and of their descendants) link two countries. Transferred from the national frame of analysis to the transnational or international frame of diasporas, their requests for legislative, regulatory, technical, and sanitary adaptations so they can have the funeral rites performed in accordance with their personal convictions and constraints, takes on a new legitimacy. They lead to the creation of public policies, and are a way of suggesting that citizenship should be redefined.

[12] bell hooks, *Yearning: Race, Gender, and Cultural Politics*, (Boston: South End Press, 1990). Gloria E. Anzaldua, *Borderlands - La Frontera. The New Metiza* 1987, (San Francisco: Aunt Lute Books, 1999).

The essay written by Amélie Nicolas and Julia Ramírez Blanco, "*Barcelona en comù*: Questions Facing a New Brand of Political Action," begins by studying the process through which the municipal government of Barcelona was taken over in May 2015 by figures from social movements under the leadership of Ada Colau, who was steadfastly determined to "deglobalize" the city. Their inquiry, which took place at the Barcelona city hall, aimed to understand the political, social, and activist trajectories of some of the elected officials and supporters of this new municipal government, as close as possible to their personal dimensions. The question of border is situated here between private citizenship, public citizenship, and the exercise of power; between activist action and institutional power; between the local scale and the international or transnational scale; and more broadly, between memory and history.

This research is linked to other work that advances the notion of a "multi-sited territory," which refers to non-contiguous spaces whose territoriality is based on the functional assemblage of several places. "*Laying claim to such a concept would be part of the movement that recognizes that the nature of contemporary territorialities is above all relational, because they can break away from the constraints of fixity, exhaustiveness, and exclusivity attributed to territories within the thought and practices linked to modernity.*"[13]

Artists have also been questioning the concept of borders for at least a decade, as we can see in Véronique Terrier Hermann's analysis in "Shooting from the Border," and in Christiane Carlut's artistic proposition in "The Invention of the North: Project for a Multimedia Platform." Within what some have called the spatial shift in art[14]—the observation of the

---

[13] Frédéric Giraut, "Multi-Sited Territory, Territorial Complexity, and Territorial Postmodernity: Operational Concepts for Tackling Contemporary Territorialities?", *L'Espace géographique*, 42.4 (2013): 293-305. (my adaptation of www.researchgate.net/profile/Frederic_Giraut/publication/278683896_Multi-sited_territory_Territorial_complexity_and_Territorial_postmodernity_a_relevant_conceptual_toolbox_for_t ackling_contemporary_territorialities/links/5583c24e08ae8bf4ba6fa23e/Multi-sited-territory-Territorial-complexity-and-Territorial-postmodernity-a-relevant-conceptual-toolbox-for-tackling-contemporary-territorialities.pdf).

[14] Irit Rogoff, *Terra Infirma: Geography's Visual Culture*, (London, New York: Routledge, 2000). Nato Thompson, *Experimental Geography*, (New York: Melville House Publishing/ ICI (Independent Curators International), 2008).

presence of numerous geographical concepts in the field of art—, the over-representation of borderlands, and the processes of hyper-territorialization seem to constitute fertile figures of it.[15] Borderline realities are the subject of a very large number of works and exhibitions.[16]

Borders are observed, represented, used, denounced and even misrepresented, and transfigured beyond binary oppositions, while exposing how the human gaze and representations are constructed,[17] and bringing to light discontinuities, spheres of influence and relationships (Border Art Workshop, Ursula Biemann, Alfredo Jaar, Aernout Mik, Ariella Azoulay, and Chen Chieh-Jen). For these artists, it is a matter of redefining practices and knowledge, and taking action in these lines, zones, strips of separation, contact, and confrontation, barriers or passageways that are permanent or mobile, continuous or discontinuous, external and internal.[18] Some of these works focus on space and explore space-time (see for instance the notion of "art-place object" defined by the geographer Anne Volvey to describe the product of an approach that investigates a field "to find/create a signification attached to that place"). Others go beyond questions of representation and push people to take action (art on the border, art born from or against the border). Still others focus on questions of exile, diaspora, migration, Creolization, and diversality.

These propositions are often built through formal and experimental inventions in which media and fictional-referential relations are intertwined. The performative dimension (Guillermo Gomez Pena) redeploys the aesthetic experience, its problematic, and

---

[15] Laurent Grison, *Figures fertiles: essai sur les figures géographiques dans l'art occidental*, (Nîmes: Chambon, 2002).

[16] We can cite, for example: *Crossing,* Kunsthallen Brandts (2012), *Général Bordure*, Quimper (2013), *Atlas critique,* Pougues-les-Eaux (2012), and *Frontières* at the Musée national de l'histoire de l'immigration (2015).

[17] Bertrand Westphal, *La géocritique : réel, fiction, espace*, (Paris: Minuit, 2008).

[18] Talk by Anne-Laure Amilhat Szary, Nantes, October 24, 2014. See also Anne-Laure Amilhat Szary, "Walls and Border Art: The Politics of Display," *Journal of Borderlands Studies* 27.2 (2012): 213-228.

the question of the political role of art. Far from always being linked to the border in its material realities, these propositions take up these questions from a more conceptual point of view, as we can see in Olive Martin and Patrick Bernier's *X et Y. Contre préfet de.... Plaidoirie pour une jurisprudence* and Camille de Toledo's project *Secession,* which offers reflections on and a shaping of European space around questions of translation, migration, and hybridization. In other words, some artists develop borderland thinking.[19] They invite us to conceive of and think about the border, while being attentive in both cases to the fact that there is another side of the border, and that it serves as much to create an inside as an outside.[20] Liminal thinking that considers the border to be a threshold instead of a barrier.[21]

These works often seek to deconstruct the notion of border by displacing it – a border is displaced, its signification can be displaced, and, for example, shift from a territorial logic to transterritorial dynamics. We can then think in terms of defrontalization, refrontalization, and transfrontalization (another way to evoke the perpetual play between deterritorialization and reterritorialization analyzed by Gilles Deleuze and Félix Guattari).

In her article, Véronique Terrier Hermann studies more specifically how cinema is linked to contemporary art and the essay film, and shows that it is a medium that proves to be as perceptual as it is reflexive, capable of tackling the complexity of these borderlands—points of encounter and rupture, boundaries that constitute national sovereignty, and geo-historical areas. Through her mapping of contradictory narratives *from* and *about* North Korea, based on the distinctive characteristics of the DMZ border, the artist Christiane Carlut stages the actual division of Korea (constitutional, emotional), its will to be

[19] Walter Mignolo, *Local Histories, Global Designs: Coloniality, Subaltern Knowledges and Border Thinking,* (Princeton: Princeton University Press, 2000).
[20] On the concept of borderlands, see Edward Soja, *Thirdspace: Journeys to Los Angeles and Other Real or Imagined Places,* (Oxford: Basil Blackwell, 1996).
[21] To counter identity - and difference-based essentialization, does not this liminal thinking tend to define identity no longer in relation to a center, but with respect to a border that separates from the Other? Whereas the border-barrier promises a potential confrontation, the border-threshold prepares an encounter. Instead of being a line that separates, the border becomes a tangent.

reunited, the complexity of the conflicting forces concerned, and the contemporary effects of Orientalism. Meanwhile, in "Our Understanding of the World is Broader than the Western Understanding of It," Emmanuelle Chérel does not study the border directly, but rather through the prism of a history of art that sheds light on entangled modernities. Her look back at a research project, which took on the form of a volume, made up of a dozen articles, colloquia, and exhibitions devoted to the political role of art, sketches out a map linking the art scenes in Senegal (and Africa) to those in France (and Europe). Through her observations, interpretations, and reflections, and by creating links between works and exhibitions from the 1970s to the present, which were inscribed in anticolonial and social struggles, Chérel's essay examines the theoretical tools of art history at the crossroads of various cultural, aesthetic, symbolic, and political realities.

CHALLENGING RESEARCH METHODOLOGIES AND POSITIONS

Renewed Research Objects

Thinking from the Border has led researchers and artists to open up new paths, such as the DMZ—a curious border object, and various forms of essay films, and to invent new protocols for their inquiries (following the dead, pushing open the doors of city hall, building a multimedia platform, connecting historicized artistic and social experiences from different places in the world). Via these processes of decentering and displacement, the researchers and artists were able to revisit certain theoretical notions and make evolve their own way of manufacturing knowledge.

"Following the Dead" partakes in the resuscitation of the social sciences—the current scientific banner that purports to work with the plurality of beings and acknowledge their specific modes of action and existence. This process may include taking account of the power to act of non-humans, as proposed by actor-network theory,[22] or to think the presence of divinities, the dead, and ghosts in other ways than simply as the passive media of beliefs.[23] This broader interest for non-humans and all living organisms seems to be significant enough to oblige us to reconsider what exactly defines humanity; that is, the very borders between humankind and all other living organisms (such as language) that have been constructed by a science that is above all anthropocentric.[24] The dead make the living act; they play a role as concrete mediators—beyond the symbolic—in social processes, which can produce complex effects such as transforming rituals, generating debates, and making laws evolve. This research on repatriations leads to rehabilitating the religious in so far as it has an inventive capacity—the devaluing of the religious question today (based on the perception of beliefs as something irrational) could be read as an effect of the disparaging discourse of modernity, which has been denounced by subaltern studies.

"Barcelona en comù: Questions Facing a New Brand of Political Action" endeavors to test out the pragmatic sociology of criticism formulated by Luc Boltanski in the context of the new Barcelona government.[25] At stake is an ethnographic protocol based on "pushing open the doors of city hall," meeting with politicians, understanding, asking questions, and which attempts to distance itself from a meta-critical approach to politics. It is by listening, in the framework of interviews, that social, political, and epistemological realities, as well as

[22] Bruno Latour, *Science in Action: How to Follow Scientists and Engineers through Society.* (Cambridge: Harvard University Press, 1987).

[23] See Elisabeth Claverie's work on the virgin *Les guerres de la Vierge : Une anthropologie des apparitions*, (Paris : Gallimard, 2003), and Vinciane Despret's works such as *Au bonheur des morts: récits de ceux qui restent*, (Paris: La Découverte, 2015).

[24] See the debates opened by the recent essay *How Forests Think: Toward an Anthropology Beyond the Human.* (Berkeley, London: University of California Press, 2013).

[25] Luc Boltanski. *On Critique: A Sociology of Emancipation,* (Cambridge, UK, Malden, MA: Polity, 2015).

those linked to the reading of history can emerge. This theoretical and critical project is then closely connected with the narration given by those directly involved. In this sense, we can understand how Judith Butler, Ernest Laclau, and David Harvey are both affective theoretical models, and useful for making a scientific or political project go forward.

Art/Human Sciences

Christiane Carlut, Emmanuelle Chérel, and Véronique Terrier Hermann's articles and research all bear witness in their own way to the fact that numerous disciplines—ethnography, sociology, geography, and history—are permeated by contemporary artistic practices.[26] As we can see on the L'invention du Nord website[27] and in Vincent Meessen's work, artists formulate hypotheses, borrow inquiry, investigation, and interviewing methodologies, compile a corpus of images, documents, and archives, think about the textual and visual narrative construction and its issues in terms of referentiality and fiction, state the author's position (between biographical data and situated knowledge). Emmanuelle Chérel focuses on the critique of modern paradigms (particularly by non-Western artists), which had led to a critique of the dominant narratives, the politics of representation, and relationships of authority, to the appearance of subjugated knowledge produced by postcolonial and decolonial studies,[28] to the emergence of new epistemologies (epistemology of diversity), to different constructions of knowledge, while questioning the various scientific regimes of truth.

[26] The figures of the artist generated in this process as ethnographer, auto-ethnographer, historian, and geographer are analyzed by Vanessa Théodoropoulou in « Histoires d'artistes, choix méthodologiques et enjeux épistémologiques », *Thinking from the Border* seminar, November 19, 2015. The term "research" has become commonplace in the field of art over the past 10 years, see Sandra Delacourt, Katia Schneller, Vanessa Théodoropoulou, *Le chercheur et ses doubles,* (Paris : B 42, 2016).

[27] http://penserdepuislafrontiere.fr/inventionnord.html

[28] Paul Gilroy, *L'Atlantique Noir, Modernité et double conscience*, (Paris : Amsterdam, 2010). Bill Ascroft, Gareth Griffiths, Helen Tiffin, *The Post-colonial Studies Reader,* (London, New York: Routledge, 1995). Ania Loomba, *Colonialism, Postcolonialism,* (London, New York: Routledge, 1998).

In the field of art history, this process has led to a rewriting of modern and contemporary art based on a rereading of relational phenomena (*travelling cultures*). This rewriting has been accentuated by the globalization of the international art scene over the past 25 years (with numerous paradoxes), and the assertion of extra-occidental art scenes. It is currently being developed internationally via the construction of a common narrative composed of multiple artistic foci (art venues, schools, collectives, and events) which have been circulating during the twentieth and twenty-first centuries via several cultures and horizons of thinking.[29] It is also a matter of identifying the displacements, decenterings, scissions, transformations, subversions, and contaminations.[30]

For Emmanuelle Chérel, these decenterings or shifts,[31] which oblige researchers to better analyze their standpoints, are also fundamentally concerned by issues related to the work mechanism invented, that is, as a contact zone (Marie-Louise Pratt) or one of negotiation (Bruno Latour). As for Christiane Carlut, borderland thinking, questions of threshold, the expression of differences of opinion, antagonisms, and controversies, non-coincidence, and difference itself can constitute methodological perspectives.[32] These approaches also fall within the scope of an ecological conception of the art world (a vision defended by the poet

[29] For example, the *Autohistorias* symposium, Villa Vassilieff, Paris, May, 2017.

[30] For example, the series of works by Kobena Mercer (ed.) *Annotating Art's Histories,* (Cambridge, MA, London: MIT Press, inIVA, 2008).

[31] The notion of decentering refers to an approach that invites us to apprehend the different places subsumed under the concept of the "global South," which challenges in theory and practice the human and social sciences as they are organized in the framework of an episteme imposed by Western society. This tension between the West, posited as a body that regulates the relationships between the different forms of knowledge at a given moment of human history, and the "Souths" illustrates this shift. In this sense, to decenter amounts to questioning the cognitive and political reconfigurations of the world since the 1980s, in particular since the end of the Cold War, in order to understand the potentials of new epistemological approaches. The "Souths" emerge both beyond the West, through attempts to spread knowledge of epistemes from other continents, and within it through the reconfigurations of academic research processes, in the critique of both the categories of domination by the universal as well as those that hypostasize, on the contrary, the particular in the demands for a new disciplinary organization that acknowledges a fair place for the "Humanities;" and finally, in the new methods for organizing knowledge about humans, which goes beyond its distribution in cultural arenas.

[32] See Dipesh Chakrabarty, Edouard Glissant, Achille Mbembe, and Walter Mignolo.

and artist Franck Leibovici[33]), who describes the work of art not as an inert artifact that is exhibited, but as an ensemble of practices, ordinary narratives, art collectives, temporalities, ethical, economic, and political decisions encapsulated in an artifact with unstable limits and inevitably linked to a cultural, social, and political context.

Some of our research has also led us to reflect on the ways in which scientific fields such as sociology and geography have reexamined the textual and narrative question, in its latest epistemological redefinition, under the influence of post-structuralist approaches, postmodern and postcolonial currents, and narrative sociology. These inquiries question once again the standpoint of researchers and consider their relationship to subjectivity, as well as fiction and imagination, while making use of research techniques that borrow tools from art.[34] For example, the reflections related in "Following the Dead in their Migrations" were transformed into a theatrical work by Monique Hervouët's theater company *Banquet d'avril*, which was performed in Avignon in 2017. Questioning the validity of the interviews conducted—the words gathered and then transcribed as a narrative to be played—, is a way of focusing the research on the gap between the perceptual process and the writing process. Blending embodied narratives with those of the study that is in progress, popular and erudite narratives, makes it possible to re-establish the major importance of a key moment in the inquiry and its subsequent reproduction. *« The time of the inquiry is one during which we follow the current of meaning, let ourselves be transported by it; it is the instant in which our feelings are amplified, reinflated, and migrate toward the public space in search of eyewitnesses. It is in the current of meaning that convictions are shared and memory is solicited. »*[35]

[33] Franck Leibovici, *(Des formes de vie)*, PACK album + 200 stickers, co-edited and published with Les Laboratoires d'Aubervilliers, Paris, 2012. http://www.desformesdevie.org/en/page/forms-life-franck-leibovici.

[34] These questions were examined in special issue 16 *La fiction et le réel* (2013) of the journal *Lieux communs,* edited by Elisabeth Pasquier and Emmanuelle Chérel.

[35] Jean-François Laé and Numa Murard, « L'enquête, l'enquêteur et la perception », in *Les Récits du malheur,* (Paris : *Descartes et Cie,* 1995)*,* 169-170.

The theatrical reproduction, which re-enacts percepts, affects, and concepts, is one possible way of addressing an audience that may include some of the study participants.[36] The sociologists engage not in the enunciation of words that are supposedly liberating for the people interviewed, who are becoming aware of their domination, rather in building times and places for disseminating the results of the inquiry in acts. It is essential to include in the research process these times for exchange, which prolong the field study, to complete this thought process that is affiliated with pragmatism and places much emphasis on emerging knowledge. The meeting between Amélie Nicolas and Julia Ramírez Blanco made it possible to engage in a new reading of the historiographical issues that characterized the inquiry at the Barcelona City Hall. Seizing upon the results of the inquiry, Julia Ramírez proposed a new perspective, based on a corpus of seven works of contemporary art that relate and extend differently the history of the coming to power of the *Barcelona en comù* group. It is a dialogue that examines and translates as much as it extends the socio-anthropological perspectives of politics, while questioning the role of art and its contemporary political implications (particularly as a place in which new forms and practices of "activism" are invented).

Self-analysis, Affects, and a Researcher's Subjectivity

Thinking from the border also means to no longer build a subject of research from afar, but instead to engage in a reflexive process, one of self-analysis, of what is transpiring, and which is built by one's personal history and the research process itself.[37] Each study calls into question a researcher's relationship to the world through the subject of the study and its construction, which originates directly

[36] See the journal *Sociologie et Sociétés,* « Sociologie narrative : le pouvoir du récit », 48.2 (2016); in particular, the article by Annick Madec , « La sociologie narrative : un artisanat civil. »

[37] See the contributions of postmodern anthropology (e.g., Gérard Althabe, Eric Chauvier). It is worth mentioning the precursory nature, in this perspective, of Michel Leiris's important work *Phantom Africa,* which dates back to 1934.

from it.[38] Such is the case of Amélie Nicolas's relationship to Spain: analyzing intimate citizenship and the role played by affects in the public sphere, she constructed her research project through a friendly relationship with a colleague in Spain, in the aim of studying issues related to intersubjectivity and interculturality.[39]

Questions of emotions and affects are particularly prevalent today in the social sphere and within the human sciences. "*Affect, at its most anthropomorphic, is the name we give to those forces – visceral forces beneath, alongside, or generally other than conscious knowing, vital forces insisting beyond emotion – that can serve to drive us toward movement, toward thought and extension […]. Indeed, affect is persistent proof of a body's never less than ongoing immersion in and among the world's obstinacies and rhythms, its refusals as much as its invitations.*" [40]

Affect is then understood as a disturbing agent[41] that calls on us to welcome the disorder of empirical experiments. To examine it would lead us to follow even the most fragile traces and tremors, that which surpasses of what is no longer contained, that which is unpredictable and would escape from and break apart taxonomic classifications.[42] Such is Emmanuelle Chérel's questioning vis-à-vis her approach to the artistic scene in Senegal and to the principle upon which she writes her articles, which is strongly connected to the different times at which she does her research in Dakar.

Can art history take account of a researcher's subjective and sensorial experience? How can in situ encounters and personal

---

[38] As Sandro Mezzadra and Brett Neilson have shown, the border must not be seen as a subject of study, but as a particular knowledge, a standpoint epistemology (Sandra Harding), which they call "the border as method."

[39] Anne Muxel, *La vie privée des convictions. Politique, affectivité, intimité,* (Paris: Presses de Sciences Po, 2014).

[40] Gregory J. Seigworth, Melissa Greg, "An Inventory of Shimmers," Gregory J. Seigworth and Melissa Greg (editors)*, Affect Theory Reader, (*London, Durham: Duke University Press, 2010), 1.

[41] Sara Ahmed "Happy object" in *Affect Theory Reader,* 43.

[42] Ahmed.

discoveries help in formulating ideas that are beyond the scope of the writing process in art history? Experiences that could, in a subsequent step in the work process, give birth to real or metaphoric dialogues, which are situated in the past and in contemporary reality. The ensemble would constitute a superpositioning of archives pervaded by multiple temporalities and spatialities (a display in which the archives would be performed) to engage in a discussion on the fuzzy borders between artistic and art history research. This approach also leads to teaching and pedagogical methods that seek to better occupy borders so as to better destabilize them. Such is the case of the singular link established with Korea by Christiane Carlut, and her problematic that is directly linked to her experience in defending the rights of foreigners. She has brought to light the two regimes of law and beliefs in the asylum application process, which echo the double affiliation (constitutional and emotional) of Korean citizens, and the will to articulate various forms of knowledge in the human sciences (geopolitical, historical, and anthropological) with personal and perceptible experiences. Here, affects and emotions function to shake the certainties that have led to the creation of Western stereotypes about this territory. Such is also the case of Véronique Terrier Hermann, who has worked tirelessly on the fringes of contemporary art, borrowing her tools of analysis from literature and cinema, depending on the case, to better grasp the artistic practices she pulls together and intertwines for various film screenings, seminars, and publications.

Building Shared Experiences

Following people, their objects and ideas in the situations they themselves encounter, and which challenge them in terms of their capacity to take action and to make a narrative, also means engaging in a multi-sited sociology, geography, and art history, a practice in close contact with the fields and contexts concerned, so that it has the capacity to provide an account of multiple narratives and situations.[43] *"Thinking from"* means

[43] See the precious work by Daniel Cefaï (editor), *L'engagement ethnographique*, (Paris: Editions de l'EHESS, 2010).

to make emerge, from the dynamics and relations of an inquiry,[44] the terms in which the worlds in which our interlocutors live can be described and recreated, and then reproduced in debate fora of which the formats, and modes of dissemination and reproduction must also be reinvented. This collective research project, *Thinking from the Border* has thus produced research that enables us to think about shared experiences theoretically, as well as about public space and the challenges of deliberation (Amélie Nicolas, Julia Ramírez Blanco), and about how common, public space can be activated beyond the circle of researchers. Christiane Carlut has generated a space of contradiction and controversy. Véronique Terrier Hermann has stirred up reflections and discussions through film screenings. Emmanuelle Chérel has organized study days and projects that bring together social actors from various networks, and the issues concerned are often concurrently debated in Senegal and France. In "Following the Dead," the interlocutors are not only linked by their religious background, but also constitute a public (as defined by Dewey) because of the fact that it is impossible for them in their host country to carry out their own specific funeral rite, especially in a context in which the application of the concept of secularism is increasingly limited (notably in France). The play is the first space that makes it exist in such a form, and through the multiple voices of personal experiences are pronounced the collective foundations required to meet the challenge of living together.

This book was published in French before an accompanying program of events,[45] which through public workshops (with guest speakers, artworks, and students), based on the presentation and exhibition of individual research approaches (archives), will enable the issues that are common to all of these research areas to be revealed at another level and to discover new strata of meaning and perspectives. Other elements of our research can be accessed on the *Thinking from the Border* website.[46]

[44] Nadia Mohia, *L'expérience de terrain, pour une approche relationnelle dans les sciences sociales*, (Paris: La Découverte, 2008).
[45] March 15-30, 2018, in the Nantes Saint-Nazaire School of Art gallery.
[46] http://penserdepuislafrontiere.fr.

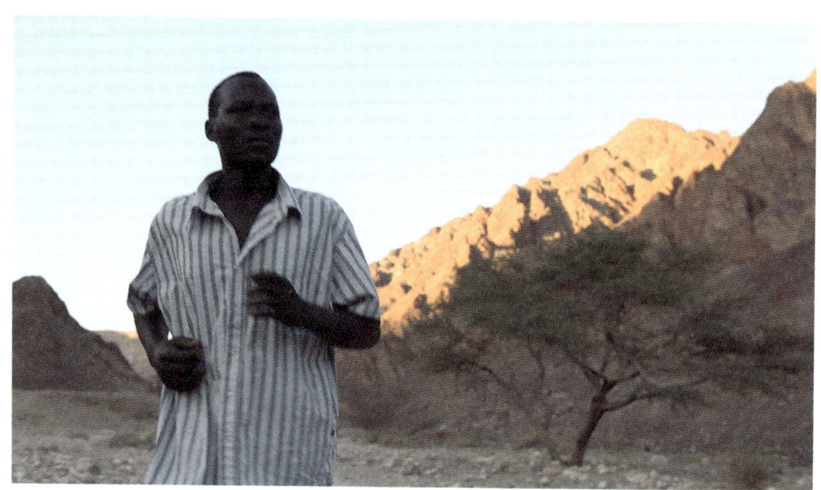

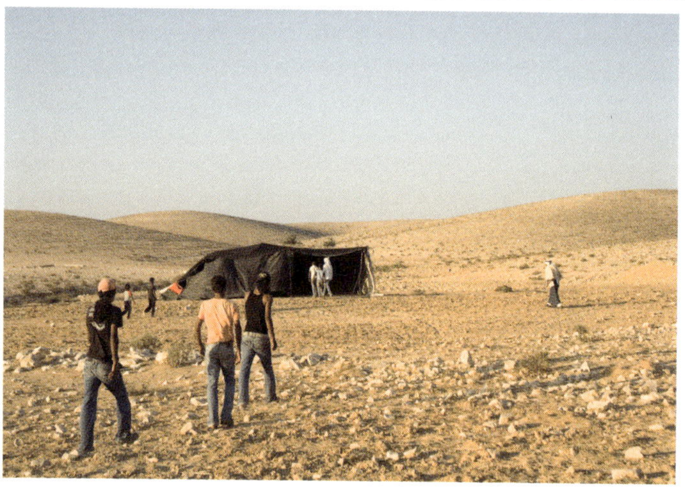

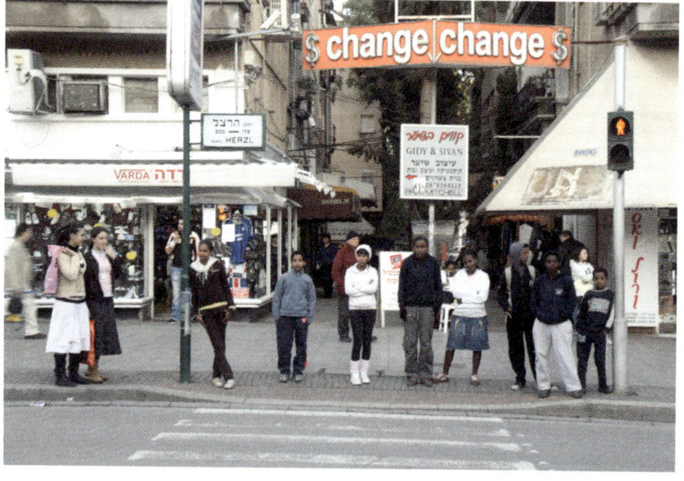
$ change change $
הרצל
HERZL
VARDA
GIDY & SIVAN
עיצוב שיער
PAUL MITCHELL

SHOOTING FROM THE BORDER

*T*aking the title *Thinking from the Border* as its point of departure, my essay will attempt to follow the lines that articulate the relationships between the border and the cinematographic works linked to contemporary art and the essay film, within the scope of issues related to questions of representation and experience.

The border has come to occupy a significant place in the field of contemporary art, which can be read at two levels. First, in terms of form—having taken up the torch from the historical avant-gardes, today's artists are actively engaged in practices that dissolve the boundaries between media through transdisciplinarity, intermediality, and transmediality. Furthermore, it is in this spirit that numerous contemporary artists have gone back to using the essay film,[1] because of the tremendous freedom in its form, as well as its capacity to blend heterogeneous elements and accommodate their will for indeterminacy between fiction and documentary. The second level at which borders occur is linked to the ways in which artists have significantly taken up again societal questions, within which border-related issues occupy an increasingly important place. In this sphere, there are many exhibitions, events, colloquia, and research programs,[2] as well as a new academic discipline called *Border Studies*.

Without disregarding the permeabilities and formal hybridizations explored in many films, and first of all in essay films, in my essay the border is defined in terms of its geopolitical dimensions and cultural impacts. Nonetheless, this very term must also be understood in all of its polysemic meanings, and even for its power to divide. A division on the ground, but also in our minds in which the term cleaves people's

[1] On the essay film, see the collective book by Bertrand Bacqué, Cyril Neyrat, Clara Schulmann and Véronique Terrier Hermann (editor) *Jeux sérieux: cinéma et art contemporains transforment l'essai*, (Geneva: Mamco/HEAD, 2015).
[2] Including the research program (*Thinking from the Border*) within which this article was written.

Assaf Shoshan, *Territories of Waiting,* (video stills), @courtesy of the artist.
Taaban, 2010, Unknown Village, 2007, Barrier, 2008.

opinions, because while from within the border can signify "protection," from without it can be perceived as an "obstacle."[3] Finally, the border is a lattice of tensions and polarities, from the outside and the inside, inclusion and exclusion, protection and the assertion of hegemony. It attracts attention and is focused on by the media and the public, which all too often influences governments to respond in an authoritarian and highly visible manner by building gates, fences, and walls.

The 2016 World Press Award was given to the photographer Warren Richardson for his singular and effective image[4] related to the current migration crisis shaking Europe. His image represents a Syrian man who is cautiously passing a baby through a razor wire fence along the Hungarian border. This shot does not represent one of those borders that is closed in response to this humanitarian crisis, nor the chaos or multitude of migrants, but a passage, only one, with great caution and attention. It focuses on a singular moment, freezes time, the time of an image, a hole in the border in search of new hope, a new life. If it is certainly an iconic image, one that is definitely effective; whereas, the films chosen for my study do not function in the same way, and do not seek to have the same impact.

For *thinking from the border* means to go beyond fascination alone—and those photogenic walls—to turn toward often less visible effects, impacts, and scars, but which these same borders have or leave everywhere and on many. It also means to problematize, complexify, and to combine the methodological approaches of the different human sciences—for if in geopolitics the border is the place of division, in anthropology, it could be examined as a meeting place.[5] *Shooting from the border* means tackling complexity, eluding the

---

[3] See the studies by Michel Foucher, a geographer, diplomat, and border expert. His works include *L'invention des frontières*, (Paris: éditions Fondation pour les études de la défense nationale, 1987) and *L'obsession des frontières,* (Paris: Perrin, 2007).

[4] See: www.worldpressphoto.org/collection/photo/2016/spot-news/warren-richardson

[5] See the works by the anthropologist Michel Agier, including *La Condition cosmopolite*, (Paris: La Découverte, 2013), the research program he directs «Babels, La ville comme frontière», http://anrbabels.hypotheses.org/, and the collection he launched in 2017, «Bibliothèque des frontières» published by Le passager clandestin.

traps of the "immediate" and iconic image, attempting new approaches and new forms of movies. The artists and documentary makers gathered in this undertaking, as if in response to the fears raised by Walter Benjamin, want to push up the value of experience.[6] In that endeavor, they did not hesitate to take the roads less travelled by, to attempt to use alternative approaches, combine sources, confront different stories, and revisit past traces. In short, they dared to make borderland cinema. Cinema made up of experiences, gazes, thoughts, and suspended, mobile, rhythmic, decentered, fragmentary, imperfect and subjective forms. Fundamentally, essay films that are engaged in a process of complexifying[7] and articulating a relationship between elements, and which do not function assuredly and definitively, but rather as people who doubt in response to the difficulties of dealing with borderland questions.

In addition, since the border is also articulated as method,[8] this text prolongs the collective experience of the movie theater. The movie schedule[9] as a work platform: show movies, connect them, compare viewing experiences, suspend or restore, for at least a short time, the movement of images; it also means to move, feel, engage one's responsibility, share and compare specific sensory experiences. My essay is composed of four movements, like four screenings: *The Wall: Issues of Representation, The Border as Place of Experience, Access Denied,* and to conclude, *The Historicity of Borders.*

[6] In "Experience and Poverty" (1933), Walter Benjamin warned us that the value of experience had plummeted, because we were becoming impoverished in terms of communicable experiences. Walter Benjamin, *Selected Writings*, Vol. 2 1927-1934, (Cambridge: Belknap, 1999).

[7] I am alluding here to the following discussion between Chantal Akerman and her famous editor, Claire Atherton, related by the latter: "Each film, each installation was like the first time. There were no rules, fears, or barriers. Every time we embarked on a new sensorial and intellectual adventure. […] I would sometimes tell her 'we need to make it more complex.' She loved *that* word. She would say: 'Yes, that's it, make it a bit more complex.' […] Making it more complex did not mean more complicated, it meant weights and counterweights, working on the dramatic tension." Claire Atherton, *Hommage à Chantal Akerman*, Online interview on the Cinémathèque française website, November 16, 2015, http://www.cinematheque.fr/article/726.html.

[8] Sandro Mezzadra and Breit Neilson, *Border as Method*, (Durham: Duke University Press, 2013).

[9] I have also proposed a series of movies *Le cinéma comme expérience de la frontière (Cinema as the Experience of the Border)*, organized for the association Contrechamp at the Cinématographe movie theater, 2014 to 2016, available online at: http://www.lecinematographe.com/CONTRECHAMP_r80.html.

The Wall: Issues of Representation

The current dynamic processes of globalization and mondialization involve the complex circulation of people, goods, and data that all require regulatory systems. Likewise, in response to the deficit in terms of the primary role played by borders, on the one hand,[10] and the crisis of national sovereignties, on the other,[11] we have been witnessing a growing transgression of them, to which governments have reacted with the same solution of closing their borders. Closed in or out by walls,[12] which are first of all veritable stages for politics, and as we must remember are not always built with the same objectives in mind: some serve to limit immigration (Europe, South Asia, USA/Mexico), others to establish a sense of security in a region (the Middle East), still others to take over a territory (Western Sahara). And what can be said about the emblematic DMZ between the two Koreas? At the same time as they built these walls, these same nation-states started deploying along the borders a technological arsenal of digital surveillance systems. This concept of *Smart Border* itself overflows the border lines, since we have been witnessing the concomitant externalization of the control and management of the current borders.[13]

Nevertheless, be it real or fantasized, virtual or concrete, the idea of the border is still mainly signified or symbolized by a wall. Such is

---

[10] See for example Régis Debray's essay, *Eloge des frontières*, (Paris: Gallimard, 2010). Debray would like to see the regulatory power of the border maintained, because it protects internal diversities, and it is opposed to the power of the wall that involves closure. He sees the border as an anti-wall. "As a good European, I have chosen to celebrate what others lament: the border as a vaccine against the epidemy of walls, a remedy for indifference, which may save life itself. I have thus written this astonishing and explosive Manifesto against the wind in my attempt to decipher our past while daring to face the future" (back cover).

[11] "It is the weakening of state sovereignty, and more precisely, the detachment of sovereignty from the nation-state, that is generating much of the frenzy of nation-state wall building today." This statement encapsulates the principle of walled sovereignty developed by Wendy Brown in her essay *Walled States, Waning Sovereignty*, (New York: Zone Books), 2010, 24.

[12] Such as the historical Roman *limes* and the Great Wall of China.

[13] Notably through the setting up of controls, monitoring, and sharing of files that concern people as well as goods, no longer only at the border itself, but at the scale of the entire Schengen area.

the case, even if the reality in the field contrasts with its strong symbolic significance—remember that in 2015, walls were only found along 4% of the total length of borders.[14] Why, then, does the wall occupy such a significant place in our collective imagination? Is it its visual presence, photogenic appeal,[15] or symbolic value that makes it such a striking figure? The answer is complex, but its very multiplicity confers upon the wall a kind of worldwide legitimacy (which is true even though its effectiveness has never been proven!), and makes the wall the *perfect response* nation-states can give their citizens, who often demand that one be built.

Such are the questions that abound in the movie *From the Other Side*[16] (2002), directed by Chantal Akerman. On the one hand, the camera captures the intimate and dramatic narratives of Mexicans who speak about their journeys, and also about those who died: "they have stories to tell… unfortunately."[17] On the other hand, her camera travels to interview Americans, mainly from the border state of Arizona, who speak about their problems in dealing with the influx of illegal immigrants. Considering that they are not protected, these people organize militias to police the border, and, due to a feeling of being abandoned by their leaders, demand themselves that a wall be built!

As is always the case for this filmmaker, it is the quality of her shots (we are in the land of Westerns) and the subtle editing that

---

[14] Michel Foucher, "for *walls* and *fences* in the strict sense of those terms, 3% to 4% of the total terrestrial borderland sheaths," « La réaffirmation des frontières », *Frontières*, (Paris: Magellan & Cie, 2015) 33.

[15] Numerous news photographs and illustrations and movie images emphasize the graphic and awe-inspiring qualities of border walls from Berlin to Jerusalem, and of course Mexico.

[16] This movie has been analyzed in detail, so I will only mention it briefly, and refer my readers to: Corinne Maury and Ángel Quintana, « De l'autre côté, de Chantal Akerman. La peur de l'autre », *Filmer les frontières*, Corinne Maury and Philippe Ragel (editors), (Vincennes: Presses universitaires de Vincennes, 2016), 33-44.

[17] In the words of Chantal Akerman, concerning her experience shooting this movie, and related by, 2015, "Over There: Chantal Akerman presents from the Other Side at FIAF," Film Comment, www.filmcomment.com/blog/over-there-chantal-akerman-presents-from-the-other-side-at-fiaf/.

render all the complexity of this borderland area. But Akerman also chooses to draw attention to the speech of individuals—each looking at the other differently—to effectively plunge us into phenomena concerning the construction of fear and the hatred of the Other.[18] For ultimately what rises to the surface of the image is indeed the confused expression and propagation of a more or less fantasized and unveiled collective unconscious, for a movie that attempts to shed light on the extent to which the border is truly a "place-symptom of the fear of the Other."[19]

— *ZONE D'INDIFFÉRENCE*

In *Zone d'indifférence* (2016), Brigitte Zieger operated in the same territories, but chose to focus her lens directly on the wall, in order to fully reveal its singularity and ambivalence. During her many stays in Arizona and New Mexico, she spent long days along the wall. Fascinated by the border patrol cars that would pass by, she monitored their constant back and forth trajectories on the dirt road along the border, their slow-motion movements, moments of waiting and keeping watch at the foot of the wall. Like a strange ballet of cars dancing to the rhythm of wheels whizzing by on a dirt road and a few bird songs, the editing produces a calm, even relaxing movie that stretches these moments of surveillance. This movie seems to unroll in nearly suspended time, denying the flow and the rhythm generally linked to the border, thereby producing a form of latency, obsolescence, and more.

But Zieger's images also focus our attention on the pattern of the wall, which snakes within the undulating landscape, and is highlighted by a red dirt road. Beautiful and unvarnished, her images unfurl a wide range of points of view of the wall, including its drop shadow and its overwhelming presence. While the construction of this part of the border took

[18] On this subject, see the movie by Antonio Muntadas, *On Translation: Miedo/Jauf*, 2007, on the construction of the fear of the Other, shot on the European/African border.

[19] Expression taken from the geographer Anne-Laure Amilhat-Szary, during her remarks at a research seminar, *Penser depuis la frontière*, 2014, Nantes.

place at several different times, it also required several different techniques. The first section was built in California within operation Gatekeeper starting in 1994.[20] It was made of large sheets of corrugated metal that were installed vertically, thus rendering it completely opaque. However, Border Patrol agents could no longer see the Mexican side of the fence, which limited their capacity to anticipate any incursions by illegal immigrants. That explains why in response to this amusing and equally cynical "revenge of the wall," Army engineers had to redesign this structure so that agents could see through it. A strange vertical architecture made of metal beams came to replace the opaque metal sheets.

Because of the time that elapsed between the different shoots, the artist could live through that transformation. In response, she decided to invert the occultation process in the images in her movie, by effacing, or rather making the Mexican landscape gray. Echoing this illusory way of eradicating the problem, the image deprives us of the other side; all the more in that this dramatic treatment of the image radicalizes the wall effect, which produces a veritable gash in the landscape that is symptomatic of the tension between the rich and the poor.

— CONFINEMENT

We all know the story. In response to the infamous "Us over here, them over there"[21] uttered by its prime minister, the Israeli government launched the construction of a border wall to protect it from its neighbors. Yet much more than a "security fence," it also contributes to a colonizing strategy. "The Wall is simultaneously an architectural instrument of separation, of occupation, and of territorial expansion mandated by the twinning of state-sponsored and outlaw extensions of settler colonialism."[22]

It is in this context that the photographer Anne-Marie Filaire made several trips to the urban zones around Jerusalem to bear witness to this colossal construction project and its impacts, and make the

---

[20] Preceded by Operation Hold the Line, and subsequently the post-September 11 Secure Fence Act (2006) allowed each border state to continue these operations or strengthen its border.
[21] Ehud Barak, Prime Minister of Israel, cited by Wendy Brown, *Walled States,* 32.
[22] *Walled States,* 35.

movie *Confinement*.[23] To render the vast length of the wall, she opted for a horizontal format in black and white, and played on the repetition of panning shots. Edited using cross fade or dissolve techniques, the images slide slowly over each other, building silent panoramas. The viewpoints chosen highlight not only the various steps in the construction of the wall (building site, marks, boundary lines, piles of materials, and machines), but also its effects on the landscape. The omnipresent wall element ends up eclipsing the activity of human beings, who are absent from the images. In some views, it marks the boundary between galloping urbanization and stagnating poverty; in others, it casts its shadow or obscures the background; in yet others, the wall literally blocks our vision, contributing to a feeling of increased anxiety and confinement.

The photographer draws, then, all of her visual demonstration from the only elements in the landscape that all converge upon this "wall effect" that she develops throughout her film. And although a separation is always differently perceived from one side or the other, her film shows that the Palestinians have no other option than to live as if it were an occupation wall that constrains and subjugates them. A "safety fence" or a "wall of shame" in the words of Wendy Brown, but more objectively, we could speak of technology for the purposes of separation and domination, and consequently, of the symbolic force of representation to which this film continuously bears witness. *Confinement* inscribes in this way the metamorphosis of the landscape as a geopolitical transformation, while its reflective power examines the methods for constructing and deconstructing our vision and imagination, and how we express history.

More generally speaking, walls have become vital elements in the strategies that have been shaping our collective consciences, fueling

[23] Anne-Marie Filaire, "The movie *Confinement* is a long tracking shot that bears witness to the closing off of landscapes, particularly those around Jerusalem. What is shown in it is time." http://www.annemariefilaire.com/.

feelings of fear on one side, and of humiliation on the other. And this is where their horrible efficacy comes to light: when they are insidiously installed as the architecture of unease, and contribute to what Edward W. Saïd called *imaginative geography*, the mental organization of space that produces identities by establishing boundaries.[24]

The Border as a Place of Experience

In counterpoint to the aforementioned works, which prefer silence, I would like to cite noisier films, in particular, because they connect borders with conflicts. *Five Broken Cameras* (2011) by the Palestinian Emad Burnat follows his stormy journey and confrontation with colonists as they continuously coerce and constrain his immediate daily activities. Five cameras that embody as many altercations in the permanent and sometimes violent conflict caused by the occupation and expropriation strategy confronting the improvising filmmaker as he tries to defend his daily environment. Filmmaking within the scope of the urgency and necessity of physical proximity that is central to direct cinema. *All Is Well on the Border Front* (1997) by the Lebanese artist Akram Zaatari uses a similar approach to focus on violent images and sounds. This film is mainly the fruit of editing work, which exploits the sonorous and visual aspects of televisual images, in order to bear witness again to a new movement by Israeli army forces to occupy southern Lebanon. These two very noisy films suggest that silence is not the only element in the processes through which geography can be deconstructed.

— *D.M.Z - MEMORIES OF A NO MAN'S LAND*

Another experience is that of border guards. The South Korean artist Hayoun Kwon uses cinema's latest immersive technologies to plunge us into the memory of a soldier stationed at the North/South border. *D.M.Z - Memories of a No Man's Land* (2015) brings us into

[24] Edward W. Said, *Orientalism.* (New York: Pantheon Books, 1978), cited by Wendy Brown, *Walled States*, 113.

this forbidden zone, which is highly guarded and monitored on both sides. Since its creation, it has gone well beyond its function as a buffer zone to become the locus of countless pains, fractures, and hopes, but also fantasies. Opting for virtual technology, which has no limits, the artist enables us to pass through the images (once the first gate has opened, the camera goes through the soldier's personal photographs, and we find ourselves in the zone), invert the perspectives (in the proper as well as the figurative sense, since the camera dives underground and then rotates in a way that enables us to walk on top of the earth again), and ultimately penetrate the entirely sublimated memory of this soldier (figured in the final surreal and magical images of fireworks). If Kwon opts for this kind of immersive experience in its fantastic dimension, it is precisely to enable us to approach as closely as possible this permanent staging of the border, as well as its widely shared power to crystallize people's imaginations.

Yet, the borderland is also the place of travelling, of transitional experiences, of the hopes of refugees and migrants in abeyance. I am thinking of the series of narrative films by Bouchra Khalili,[25] which entail questions of travelling, wandering, and quite often *failure*. However, while borderland questions are manifest in all of her work, viewers' attentions are drawn to imaginations that certain territories arouse. For *The Mapping Journey Project*, the narratives related are those of migrants who have given up or were rejected at the border. The visual sequences show a tightly framed map on which a hand draws the person's migratory journey, and function as the material support for a voice-over narrative of an aborted expedition. The power of the film's protocol is how it makes the map itself a screen-image, uniting its flat materiality with the mental projection of a place somewhere else.

Shooting from the border also means to envision it in its waiting zones: encampments and camps, from the interfaces of these waiting

[25] Bouchra Khalili, *Straight Stories* (2006-2008), a series of narratives in ambiguous border zones in the Mediterranean Region, and *The Mapping Journey Project,* 2008-2011, maps of clandestine journeys.

zones to places of transit, to improvised jungles[26] on migratory routes. The first least visible ones are the "reticular zones," which have emerged from the need to control borders, such as the international zones set up in airports by the border police. These detention zones, where the number of detainees is highly variable, are difficult to connect with the transit places concerned, and produce countless formalities, aberrations, and paradoxes. Here too, cinema finds food for thought. The filmmaker Nicolas Klotz made a lengthy stay at Charles de Gaulle Airport to create his fictional film *La blessure* (2003).[27] Another observation of these waiting zones can be found in *Transit* (2004) by the artist Taysir Batniji. Furtively shot footage—particularly because it is forbidden to take photographs—, he documents the transit zone for Arab populations that cross the Gaza/Egyptian border. Simple and effective, the film is pieced together like a slide show, a succession of images of people waiting, of discrimination, and of the ordinary humiliation of such people.

The second kind of waiting zones, the encampments, are areas that emerge along major migration routes or near border cities. They crop up spontaneously and are often self-managed and changing: they can be established on a long-term basis, if they receive support from humanitarian associations and are approved by the country. In France, we can think of the former camp at Sangatte, which was subtly filmed by the artist Laura Waddington, who showed us its fragility, as well as the violence and terror that reigned there. Her film, *Border* (2004), presents a series of fuzzy and jerky images of border police officers chasing migrants in the dark night near this jungle camp. In *Qu'ils reposent en révolte* (2011), the director Sylvain Georges films in the city of Calais itself, but after the jungle, when the migrants are being dispersed. His camera seeks them out in the city, where their existence is ordered by the quest to satisfy their basic needs and the necessity to live in hiding. Scorned by many inhabitants, constantly subjected to

[26] From the jungle in Calais, France to the one in Choucha, Tunisia.
[27] See, Leila Ennaili's study of this film in « La Blessure de Nicolas Klotz ou la face cachée de la frontière », *Filmer les frontières*, 105-118.

police surveillance, and also stalked by extremist factions, the filmmaker draws a spine-chilling portrait of wandering shadows. And because they attempt to show us that which is unbearable, these two films combine a powerful cinematographic esthetic with a regard that is perforce political.

Finally, regarding the camps set up by countries or humanitarian organizations, the directors Ala Eddine Slim, and Ismaël and Youssef Chebbi infiltrated such waiting zones that had become veritable places to live. Their film, *Babylon* (2012),[28] gives us access to the daily life in the Choucha camp in southern Tunisia, on the Libyan border. Filming this place as the first migrants were arriving, it provides an account of the birth and occupation of what we must call a *de facto* city. A new kind of urban development.

— *TERRITOIRES DE L'ATTENTE*

The video installation *Territoires de l'attente* (2010) by the artist Assaf Shoshan brings together three short films that each use various forms of staging to evoke borderland experiences.

Taaban, (2010), on a first screen, filmed with a fixed camera, presents viewers a close-up shot of a man running in the desert. He is alone, and is not fleeing, however he is running, out of breath, and exhausted, as night falls. Very quickly, through a subtle visual effect, we realize that the landscape is not changing, that this character is not going anywhere, that he is literally "running in place." Irrevocably, his race will lead him nowhere—an allegory of an endless journey with no place of arrival.

On the final screen, *Barrier* (2008), filmed in the city of Israël, a static sequence shot frames people on a pedestrian crossing, but gradually we notice that some do not step off the sidewalk. Those who remain on it, as if prevented by an invisible border, are Jews of Ethiopian origin, the very people that the Promised Land does not welcome exactly like the others. The film resonates with the

28 This film won the Grand Prize in the international competition at the FID Marseille in 2012.

phenomenon of "differential inclusion" alluded to by Mezzadra: *"Not only are migrants at the same time within and without, the elusive border between interior and exterior, between inclusion and exclusion, has become crucial in the lives of a multitude of other subjects."*[29]

And between the two, the film *Unknown Village* (2007) frames a landscape in the Negev desert. A small group of men walk toward a black tent planted in the center, and then more, and even more. Some arrive alone, on foot, on donkey, and even by car, but they all take shelter progressively in the tent. A dark mark in the golden landscape, this strange, indistinct shape is at the same time a refuge for the Bedouins and a passageway for the nomads, as well as a trap for the migrants, like a black hole, a place of no return; for this shapeless pocket in which these men continually pour without ever exiting, also arouses unconscious and even childlike fears, like a giant mouth engulfing these tiny men.

Territoires de l'attente draws its force from the allegorically evocative force of each video, as well as their proximity. Whatever their perspective may be, they all converge towards the same hope that is always thwarted, always obstructed, always annihilated.

Access Denied

"In this atomic age of speed, we are shut in and shut out by passports!". Already in *A King in New York* (1957), Charlie Chaplin reminded us of the ambivalent role of our passports, which provide us access or shut us in our countries. In today's world—no longer the atomic age but the omni-digital age—, countries have developed the concept of *smart border,* which aims to respond with technology to the ever-increasing need to control our borders. At the same time, a

[29] Sandro Mezzadra, interview in French in *Vacarmes*, October 2014, accessed on-line version in April 2017, http://www.vacarme.org/article2682.html.

principle of externalization and delocalization of regulation and surveillance systems gives new virtual borders the possibility to act everywhere and at any moment. For example, in the Schengen area, the controls take place before the crossing points, in the countries of origin or transit, but also after the fact when illegal immigrants are intercepted. The visible part of the increasingly powerfully computerized borders is embodied in the deployment of cameras and drones, as well as sensors, scanners, and virtual fences, which all serve a technology of surveillance and detection. A veritable connected network reinforced by intelligent documents—digital, biometric, and satellite files, and the monitoring and sharing of information, which concerns people as much as goods—, the border is now perceived to be an ensemble of more or less visible, but constantly activable data.

On the eve of the twenty-first century, the artist Ursula Biemann had already pointed out the links between surveillance and digital technology on the border between the United States and Mexico in *Performing the Border* (1999).[30] "The border technologies and those for monitoring work installed in Juarez establish relationships between vision, surveillance, power, and violently present bodies" writes the artist.[31] A veritable inquiry within a feminist perspective, the film problematizes the border in its relations with the economy, computing, prostitution networks, and crime.

— *CENTRO DI PERMANENZA TEMPORANEA*

Adrian Paci's film, *Centro di Permanenza temporanea* (2007) focuses on the relationships between bodies and surveillance technologies. Albanian and living in Italy, Paci is very sensitive to the question of borders: "The fact that I am at the crossroads of different paths, at the boundary between two separate identities, can be found

[30] See the presentation of this film on the artist's website: www.geobodies.org/art-and-videos/performing-the-border.
[31] Ursula Biemann, « Performing the border. Sur le genre, les corps transnationaux et la technologie», *Multitudes*, Paris, n° 15, 2004, www.cairn.info/revue-multitudes-2004-1-page-75.htm.

in all of my cinematographic productions."[32] While the title clearly points out the euphemistic name given to these migrant shelters, his film makes use of the familiar routine of travelling in an airplane to highlight its limits, the invisible shapes that differentiate, unite, and exclude individuals according to their nationality. Indeed, we see men and women walk toward and up ramp stairs as if to board a plane. The camera then takes the time to sketch a thoughtful portrait of each of them, and then of the group, crammed together at the end of the ramp stairs, for an endless wait. When the camera starts moving again, it zooms out to reveal the emptiness of what is beyond the frame. No airplane, no trip, no border crossing, no job on the other side… Nothing but an invisible and inflexible selection, a definitive wait on a tarmac with no future. Shooting from the border often engages with flow and movement, but in this case, the entire film stages the construction of a suspended figure, frozen in its final movement, at the height of its impediment. Nevertheless, more than just a portrait of a group of excluded people, the film is a plural and multiple portrait, because the camera conserves the singularity, quality and personal force of resistance of each individual, as if neither waiting nor exclusion can dissolve any of them into the mass of the excluded.

— *AS THE COYOTE FLIES*

Adrien Missika is an artist-voyager-explorer, but in its contemporary version, which means in the age of a world duplicated in visual and exploitable data. He endeavors to undermine certain codes of representation, by composing his works in relation to the limit between the visible and visibility. With his film *As the Coyote Flies* (2014), shot at the Mexican border, he turns surveillance technologies against themselves. Indeed, the artist launches a drone equipped with a camera, in eleven attempts to illegally fly over the border between Juarez City and the Pacific coast. *As the Coyote Flies*, because

32 Adrian Paci, « Vies en transit », press release, Jeu de Paume, 2013.

"coyote" is the name generally used to refer to people smugglers, but in this case, it is a drone, a technological tool generally used to monitor the border. Embarked in this way, the camera provides us beautiful views of the wall, the surrounding areas, roads, and even the first villages, while the quality of the rather awkward and chaotic aerial images, contrasts with the idea of a *smart border*. In addition, the sequential editing of the eleven flights gives us a counter image of this zone that is commonly said to be subject to tension, and preoccupies Americans so much: No illegal immigrants, no attacks by illegal aliens, hardly any surveillance (we can make out two or three border patrol officers on duty, who are very small in the image, two of whom are looking up at the drone). Ultimately, everything seems to be quite peaceful, we might even say in contradiction with the vision that justifies the growing necessity of surveillance, control, and closing the border, which is so common in the United States. In its playful dimensions, this film thus pokes fun at the vulnerability and perhaps the amorality of the exponential development of the means for policing borders—a simple message that may potentially apply to other places in the world.

Historicity of Borders

Borrowing, according to their needs, from anthropologists, geographers, and historians, several artists remind us of the history of borders; some even embarking upon a search for former borders that have more or less disappeared. I am thinking of the film by Pauline Delwaulle and Clément Postec, *Linescape* (2010), a travelogue of their field investigations during which they search for the border line of the former Bosnia-Herzegovina, but also of *Kamen—Les pierres*, (2014) by Florence Lazar, made in former Yugoslavia. This territory was mistreated, wounded, cut up and crossed by borders, and subject to religious divisions, and in these processes a certain number of traces of these different passages and occupations were imprisoned and sedimented. The artist then turns her camera toward these lands, rocks, and silent stones that she sounds out through the very people who know how to make them speak, and she enables us to see multiple revampings and rearrangements of ruins, which go as far as the fabrication of an alternate history at the scale of a city. Taking on the role of an observer, she makes use of cinematographic means to reveal these controversial arrangements with History.

Elsewhere, Francis Alys, made a video *The Green Line* (2005) that bears witness to his performance. In it we see the artist during one of his strolls in Jerusalem, discretely leaving behind a green line painted on the demarcation line established after the 1948 Arab-Israeli War, a simple gesture, but one which attempts to remake History a bit more visible.

— *ROUTE 181, FRAGMENTS OF A JOURNEY IN PALESTINE — ISRAËL*

A duo of Israeli-Palestinian filmmakers, Eyal Sivan and Michel Khleifi, decided to undertake a voyage along this same border demarcation line in *ROUTE 181 — Fragments of a Journey in Palestine-Israel* (2003). This border line was drawn by the United Nations to pacify the zone, but far from putting an end to the conflicts, instead Israel has kept nibbling away at territories, evicting individuals, and redrawing landscapes. Following this line, is thus an attempt, through cinema, to call into question a land-based affiliation or heritage. Throughout their trip, the filmmakers reveal as many vestiges of Arab civilization in the landscape as traces of the current occupation, and meet as many people who have a story to tell, things to show, tensions to express and provoke, as others who are more resigned to silence. Nevertheless, while some are still seeking in it the traces of a bygone era, others want to find instead proof that justifies their current occupation; because that which constituted a border at one time had disappeared, nobody can truly be entirely on one side or the other. The film, which runs on for nearly four and a half hours, takes the time needed to listen, compare points of views, stories, and perspectives.

A travelogue open to any encounter or event, the film is constructed in an ongoing negotiation with the places, objects, and people filmed. Accepting its fragmentary, unfinished, impure, and even dualistic qualities, the filmmakers do not hesitate to increasingly complexify the historicity of these lands that have been so mistreated and scarred.

—ONCE I ENTERED A GARDEN

Another filmmaking duo—this time the Israeli filmmaker Avi Mograbi and his Palestinian friend Ali Al-Azhari—embark upon a visit of former Palestinian land in *Once I Entered a Garden* (2002). The force of this film resides in the fact that confronted with a moving border, which cuts across territories and individuals, and modifies history and geography, we continue nevertheless to share and to tell stories. That is a very clear manifestation of the power of the storyteller alluded to by Walter Benjamin,[33] which is expressed in the necessity to share stories and experiences, even when some people are caught up in History that is constantly marked by conflicts, resolutions, and aborted peace processes. And since this film, through its intimate camera work, becomes a conversation, we also take time ourselves to listen to the stories. We hear Avi Mograbi's dream—the story of a couple separated by the border, which maintains a correspondence through Super 8 filmed "letters"—the respective memories of two friends, their reflections on the politics of their countries, marked by the guilty feelings of the Israeli filmmaker, but also their bondedness and quarrels. We even delight in dreaming of a Middle East without borders, to which some of their stories allude. Yet one sequence is utterly shocking, because it does not allow us to tell any more stories, arousing only indignation. During one of their outings, to be precise in Ali's former village, his daughter goes to play in a garden. Very quickly, she comes upon a sign written in Hebrew that says "foreigners forbidden." She is completely discountenanced at first, and wants to leave immediately,

[33] See Walter Benjamin "The Storyteller" (1936), in *Walter Benjamin: selected writing. Vol. 3. 1935-1938* (London: Belknap, 2006).

then, in a second phase, needs to return there and physically express her youthful anger by kicking the sign. Once we have watched the scene, we understand that the film itself needs to return to this sequence, to make, not a return to the past through images, but to harness the self-reflexive means of cinema, and in particular the spoken word and thought,[34] in order to digest what we believed was a bygone era.

— *TERRES VAINES*

Searching for borders that have disappeared, the film *Terres vaines* (2012), by Augustin Gimel and Brigitte Perroto, unfolds in a cinematic-poetic mode. It is a very visual work, with impeccably filmed landscapes, accompanied by the reading of a text by the writer Alexandre Koutchevsky.[35] Through their traces and vestiges, the landscapes concerned evoke ancient histories, those of countries that have disappeared or moved their borders. The movie camera follows the ruins of Hadrian's Wall in the heart of England, which used to mark the limits of the Roman Empire. Elsewhere, the camera takes a trail that emerged from the furrow left behind by the iron curtain that used to divide Germany. While the writer's text takes root in the cracks at these sites through snapshots of individuals, the film summons History, or at least, the historicity of all of the traces, marks, and scars born by all landscapes.

These reminiscences of borders constitute our History, just as they mark a certain attachment of populations to territories, but far from immobilizing or diminishing this History, they bear witness at the same time to the countless movements and flows in which populations have always participated. In addition, the film is only one part of a research and collection project carried out by these artists

[34] With the young girl no longer present, the two filmmakers discuss this sign, as much in terms of the numerous ways it echoes with History, as of her reaction to it, which conveys a double identity.
[35] Alexandre Koutchevsky is a writer and director who has made several works (particularly in airports), in which deambulation plays a central role.

concerning these ghost (or vanished) borders. It is situated within the scope of an installation and a website project, which brings together documents, treatises, and an entire iconographic ensemble that ranges from maps to medals and stamps. All of these documents redraw forgotten regions and ephemeral countries, or instead attest to conquests of territories, and inevitably occupations and colonization. This work does not so much involve the inversion of perspectives, as of thinking from the very history of borders.

Shooting from the Border

Shooting from the border would seem to weave together all of these voices and ways of looking, by including all they provide and lack, their strengths and weaknesses. For *shooting from the border* is not only a matter of deciding to make (or not to make) an image, to gaze from within or from without, but to exploit workaround strategies and visual shifts, until we can break free from the obvious authority of the image of a wall or other clichés so often associated with borders. It also means not being afraid of being subjected to contradictions and dissonant voices, daring to remain at a possible breaking point.

Thinking from the border, then, necessarily engages us to think through the prism of postcolonial theories—at a crucial and vulnerable moment when History was reassessed and responsibilities redefined —, but also through what is increasingly repressed, made up of fear of the Other and the anxiety of the former powers that see themselves weakening in comparison to the emerging countries, all of which is playing out against the backdrop of a worldwide migratory crisis. It is in this context that such essay films, free to use all the tools, methods, and forms available, can astutely complexify their approach, and in this process create possible entry-ways and subjective gazes, and make contributions—all pertinent but never definitive—, which may make *thinking from the border* possible.

Finally, there is the image from one last film, *Border/Borders* (1999), by the Turkish artist Hale Tenger. On a first horizontal screen, children are playing jump rope on a beach. Two of them are swinging the rope over which the others jump, while the movement of the waves regularly effaces the mark left behind by the rope on the sand. On a second parallel screen, the same children are playing tug-of-war. After having marked a center line, the two teams at the ends of the rope start pulling, until one of them is pulled across the center line. Movement, jumping, passing, tension, risk, moving a line, the ebb and flow of the sea… all of these elements help to construct in their own way an allegory of the border, understood in its polysemy and complexity.

In conclusion, I would like to quote the slogan of the Mexican immigrant rights movement, which, beyond its reference to the expansion of the United States onto former Mexican land, is a reminder for all of us that borders move:

"We didn't cross the border, the border crossed us!"

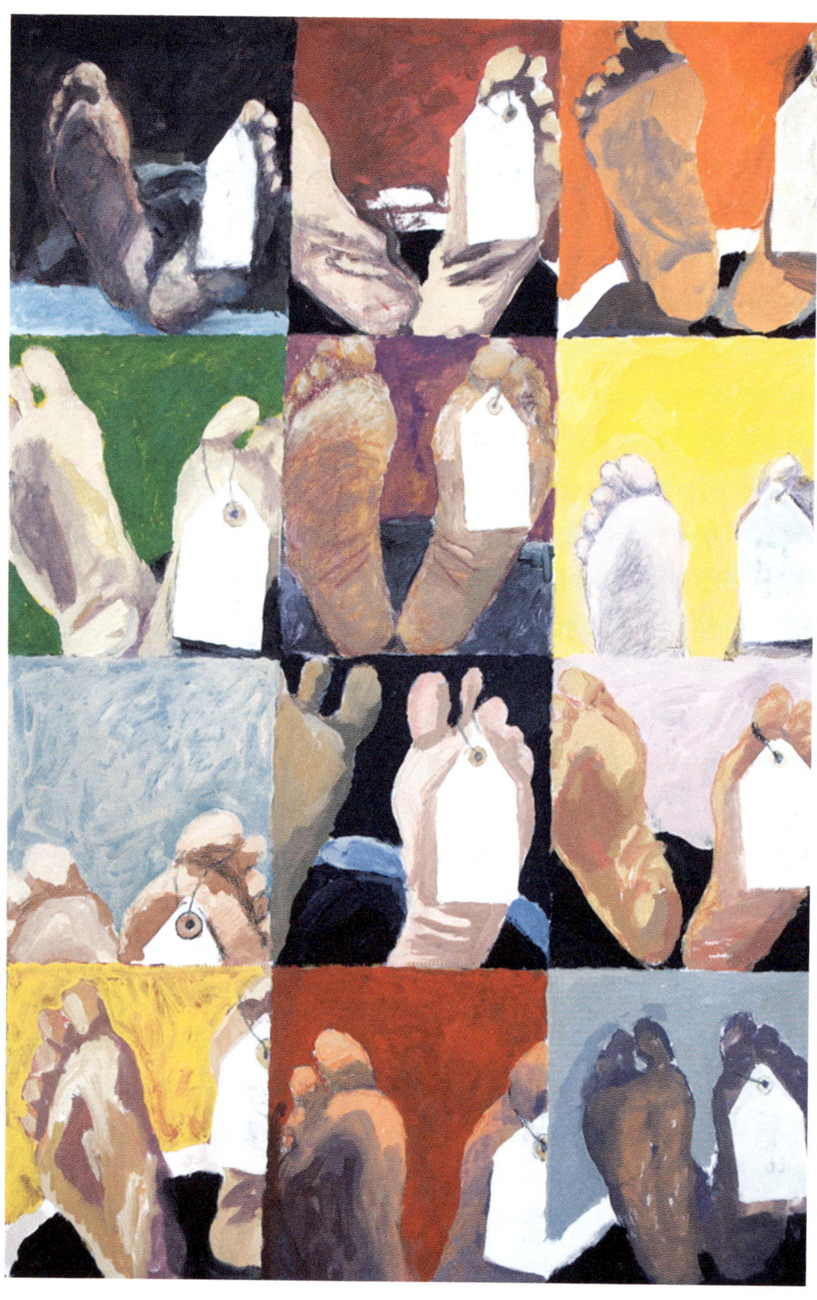

Vonnick Caroff, *Following the Dead*, painting, 2017, @courtesy of the artist.

FOLLOWING THE DEAD IN THEIR MIGRATIONS:
A TRANSNATIONAL INQUIRY

Our sociological inquiry "Following the Dead" concerns the repatriations of the bodies of migrants, and of their descendants who lived in France, to their home country for inhumation.[1] Focusing on people of Turkish, Algerian, and Moroccan descent has enabled us to continue our research on Islam as it is practiced in France today, which initially studied the construction of mosques.[2] Our method consisted in following these dead travelers in order to see what they make the living do, and to understand what plays out in this odd voyage. Conferring upon the dead the capacity to take action, that is making others do things, means to acknowledge the multiple modes of existence of beings, as the researcher Vinciane Despret invites us to do. Based on this theoretical grounding, our inquiry gave special attention to transnational rituals and to border effects, to family relations in contemporary migratory flows, as well as to the roles played by companies, States, and associations in this circuit of coffins. The transnational can then be thought of as a daily product, through the actions of individuals who, as they move, move with them their religions, former and future family ties, and their know-how, while making new demands on their host country. Our inquiry reveals, for example, in France the effects of these demands on legal, technical, and sanitary modifications made by Muslims so they can carry out

[1] For this research, about thirty interviews were conducted between January, 2014 and July, 2016 with various professionals (funeral homes, repatriation companies, a doctor from the medical emergency services at the Roissy airport, employees of the Nantes University Hospital mortuary service and the Nantes municipal cemetery service), and with people who had repatriated a close friend or family member to their home country.

[2] That research analyzed the negotiations between the people involved through a comparison of three cities in the Pays de la Loire Region. Cf., Anne Bossé, Elisabeth Pasquier, « L'espace public dans les Pays de la Loire au contact de l'islam » Languages, Urban Actions, Alterities Laboratory at the Nantes Graduate School of Architecture, funded by the Pays de la Loire Région, January 2013.

their funerary rituals in accordance with their convictions. It examines the relationships between integration, secularity, and the choice of being repatriated.

The subject matter of this inquiry was used to create the play *Following the Dead. Theater and the Social Sciences.*[3] The issues linked to repatriation the questions raised by this process on the management of diversity in France and the representations of death , are central to the project of making a theatrical work with the subject matter of this inquiry. Research must create forms as much as it produces objects.[4] And if theater is to a large extent a space of fiction, in our project the aim is to arouse the interest of theater spectators for the issues in today's world as conveyed by the human and social sciences. The challenge facing this collaborative project is to manufacture a specific dramaturgy, form of writing, and staging, such that each performance of the play results in a shared experience of a manifest Real.

The Repatriation Route: Embodied Logistics

The transit of a repatriated body makes it pass from unknown hands that may perform cleansing, mortuary care, and ceremonial ablutions, into the hands of family members in the home country, some of whom the deceased had perhaps not seen for a long time. For this specific corpse, those who care for the body, technical and logistics intermediaries, close friends and family are all links in a process that transports the body from where it dies to where it will be inhumed. To the time frame imposed by the natural process of degradation of this body made of biologically active matter are added the administrative times of the two States concerned, that of the funeral ceremony with its

[3] *Following the Dead: Theater and the Social Sciences.* Created by the *Banquet d'avril* theater company. Text: Anne Bossé and Elisabeth Pasquier. Director: Monique Hervouët. Starring: Karim Fatihi, Gilles Gelgon, and Delphine Lamand. Scenography: Yohann Olivier. Costumes: Anne-Emmanuelle Pradier. Production April 2017. Currently touring.

[4] cf., : http://www.laviedesidees.fr/Les-formes-de-la-recherche.html.

specific constraints according to the religion concerned, as well as the affective time for family and friends during which the body, still with no sepulcher, seems to remain in the land of the living.

During this transit time, the deceased will have generated paperwork, identity papers, administrative forms authorizing its passage between two States, documents proving it respects the sanitary rules imposed by the States on corpses, and those concerning the air transport of the body. It will have gone from a body conceived as a physical shell that must be cared for to a body referred to as human remains, and for which what counts above all—once it is in the freight process at the airport—is its length, volume, and weight. The coffin will have already been sealed, so that it cannot be re-opened (and used for the illegal transport of other goods), and is a particular coffin, designed for air transport that must be pressure resistant, and feature a very thin hermetically sealed aluminum liner. The coffin is placed in an unmarked cardboard box so that it cannot be recognized, but an employee of an international repatriation company, who was interviewed in the framework of our study, mentioned that nobody is fooled by this desire to make it inconspicuous. It speaks, however, to the impossibility of making a coffin a completely ordinary freight package. Indeed, a coffin in the baggage hold is not just any kind of merchandise. The regulatory impossibility for a HUM (*human remains*) to be placed next to perishable goods such as flowers, animals, and eggs that are about to hatch, is used as a justification by several airlines companies to refuse to transport coffins.

In addition to the infected corpse that may transmit an epidemic, as is visible in some regulatory standards still in force, and which are mixed with forms of superstition, there is the corpse that is religiously impure as long as it has not been given the necessary ablutions and prayers. States then have policies that can cause problems for repatriation companies: the embalming requirements before transport, which are repudiated by the majority religion of the destination country.

Besides these administrative formalities generated by crossing a border, which benefit the experts in this business sector linked to the globalization of flows and exchanges, who sell their services as competent technical intermediaries, the circulation of dead bodies seems to run smoothly. Only on rare occasions does it lead to blockages (when a bribe can be requested in some countries to let the body enter the territory). The airport can thus be seen as a node for the worldwide circulation of corpses. Relegated to the freight service, this circuit is of course hidden from the living passengers, but it is efficient, and possible, in every direction, to all destinations. It can concern those who are repatriated and tourists, expatriates and globalized travelers from all walks of life. In this regard, the border is less of an impassible barrier than an operator, because it transforms the bodies and objects that cross it.[5]

These functional aspects, without being what counts the most in the conveyance of a body, express various aspects of its ritualistic specificities. The particular precautions taken in anticipation of any bad surprises permeate the memories of those who organize the departure: a common thread in the narratives gathered concerns what had to be done and organized after a person dies. Surprisingly, the professionals speak more about the affective aspects than the technical ones—the pressure coming from the families, and in particular how fast they want the body to be delivered, because another part of the family is waiting on the other side of the border, is combined with the anguish caused by any trip in which there obviously remains some amount of uncertainty. There are difficulties linked to sending off the body rapidly, in finding seats for family members in an airplane that will arrive before or at the same time as the body, as well as the fear that the coffin may be lost as suitcases sometimes are. Death always takes us by surprise, even when we know it is imminent. It is crucial to arrive on time, be there at the moment of passage, which is true in both directions: when we return home in time to

---

[5] Anne-Laure Amilhat has developed the notion of *borderity* to insist on our increasingly individualized relationships to borders, in which what they do to the body (particularly those of the migrants who attempt to cross them) is a striking example. *Qu'est-ce qu'une frontière aujourd'hui*, (Paris: PUF, 2015).

see a living relative one last time, or make a relative from a country come urgently when the oncologist announces that an exiled member of the family is about to die. In the case of repatriations, while the emergency effect complicates things, we should not forget that our travel skills are well honed: the repatriation of a body is the continuation of our migratory lifestyles, and purchasing a plane ticket is a common practice with which we are familiar.

The airport is a specific threshold for families as well as various professionals. The passage through customs, which frees the international repatriation company of its responsibility, echoes with the passing on of the body from the family over here to the family over there—until this transition, the former alone was responsible for making sure the trip progressed at the right speed. To the weight of the inert body that must be transported, corresponds the heavy responsibility of the repatriated individual who when alive expressed the desire to go back, which must be accomplished as well as possible. In its capacity as a borderland, the airport produces changes in the status of the body, but it also gives the trip a particular tone for those close to a deceased individual. It is like an antechamber, which concentrates the time spent crossing the border and becomes the space of a family reunion, of reunions *via* the body. This voyage, especially for those close to the deceased individual, can elicit questions of identity and play a role in redefining affiliations. Administrative and technical issues sometimes symbolize these upheavals: for instance, the passport lost by a deceased individual who crosses the border is also the passport corresponding to the double nationality for which their daughter or son are no longer sure of reapplying.

Playing with Borders, Dealing with the Sky

How exactly do the living go about handling this double death that unfolds in two times and places? Funeral rituals, like any other rituals, are highly symbolic formalized acts, and we can acknowledge that death summons such acts more than any other moment in our lives. Our recourse to ritualized gestures, objects, and ways of behaving, are vital for keeping death at a distance, and accompany the passage and the various aspects of this moment of transition for the dead as well as the living. Ritualistic inventions and hybridizations are bound together, on both sides of the border, through the deceased individual. By means of the instructions to be repatriated they left behind on their will when they were alive, the dead seal a "compact of understanding" between two parts of a family. This transnational situation leads them to make particular arrangements: objects and practices are shaped to guarantee the passage of what must be conserved or continued from one State to the other. For example, the coffin used for the purposes of repatriation often has a small glass window, which can be concealed or opened and enables people to see the face of the deceased individual. Thanks to this adaptation, when the corpse arrives friends and family can make visual contact with the dead person.[6]

For Muslims, inhumation in the home country stirs up questions related to the land in its material dimensions, since the body is going to return to it, but also to the soil of the village and that of the country, of the nation as it is defined by its borders, as well as sacred land, the Land of Islam, where prayers for the deceased will be said by a great number of worshippers, thus annulling its belonging to a minority religion.[7] Yet, the repatriation of the deceased to the Land of Islam, in the name of religious beliefs, obliges Muslims to re-examine some of their convictions. The way the body is prepared due to the legal constraints of repatriation, with a series of specific requirements, can indeed be contradictory with Muslim funerary traditions. First of all, that of the timing, as expressed in the maxim: "you die in the morning and are buried in the afternoon," as

[6] Yassine Chaïb refers to this moment of coming face to face with the deceased as "envisagement," with which he draws a parallel concerning the often very long absence of the emigrant in « Le rapatriement de la dépouille mortelle chez les immigrés maghrébins en France, » *L'Autre*, 2006/3 (vol. 7): 399-411.

[7] The question of the preferences in relation to where immigrants are buried is highly correlated with religion; a statistical inquiry conducted in 2003 showed there is a stronger preference for inhumation in the home country among Muslims. Claudine Attias-Donfut, François-Charles Wolff, « Le lieu d'enterrement des personnes nées hors de France, » *Population* 2005/5 (vol. 60): 813-836.

well as the recourse to embalming, which is contrary to the interpretation of the Koran according to which it is forbidden to violate the physical integrity and wholeness of the dead body.

The families explain that they find themselves confronted very quickly with having to stray from the norms. We observe that repatriation manufactures a multi-site ritual—while it takes place at two times, it also occurs in two places, which enables a kind of "double presence" of close friends and family, at chosen steps in the funeral ceremonies.[8] Prayers in France can be voluntarily interrupted and then finished in Algeria. The continuity of the ceremony is achieved through the transmission of the body: the prayers are resumed once the body has crossed the border—there is simply a shift in time. Sometimes the meal that takes place 40 days after the burial is organized in France and not in the country of entombment, which enables those who could not attend the funeral services to take part in the ritual.

The border does not prevent continuity, which is stitched together through the concerted joint actions of different individuals. It is conceived of as a resource that people activate. The differentials created by the border are indeed central to the appraisals made by migrants regarding their choices for the deceased. Exercising the mobility rights of the dead,[9] is a way of challenging the dominant conceptions and/or ideologies as much of the host as of the home country; it means choosing among several places assigned to the (different) dead and therefore opting for a conception and the current norms of funerary rituals (regulatory, financial, and institutional constraints). While the repatriation of a body and the funeral ceremonies cost about the same amount as inhumation in France, the expenditures do not break down in the same way, and each part of the budget has a symbolic value. The airplane ticket is definitely more of a burden; however, the commercial logic is largely concealed

[8] The people we interviewed did not mention the use of communication technologies, but we know that funeral services can be followed on Facebook.

[9] For contemporary reflection on the freedom of movement of the dead, and in particular the new controls imposed by the French State, cf., Arnaud Esquerré, *Les os, les cendre et l'État*, (Paris: Fayard, 2011).

behind the moral virtues of an indispensable ritualistic act that has no price: the long-awaited and desired return. Economically speaking, the price of the voyage is offset by a free burial spot in the village forever. This investment is more profitable than a free inhumation in France with a five-year rental or one that you pay for and is renewable for 15 or 30 years. The definitive access to a free tomb is often compared to the funerary practices in France, a country that does not provide a perpetual tomb for its dead, and even refuses to let them rest in peace, since exhumation is not only permitted, but can be an obligation.

These repatriations express the complex relations with Islam that exist, powerful relationships around issues concerning the final voyage, since it involves finally going to paradise, but also agreeable, nuanced and tolerant relations, made up of small arrangements in the transitional zone, hybrid transformations, moments of overplayed and unsaid things, with humor expressed in the middle of tears. Language plays a major role in all of these singular, final moments: the repatriations give rise to narratives, which are indispensable for making bonds with those who are absent, either on one or the other side of the border. The transnational syncretic rituals that are invented throughout the history of repatriations would seem to play a role in changes in belief systems, relaxing rules, and a tolerant and inventive globalized Islam.[10]

Repatriation of the Dead: An Analytical Socio-cultural Tool

The dead are writing a page of the history of immigration, and the choices related to funerary rituals reveal a new facet of the long-term effects of these transnational lives. The repatriation of bodies is a key moment for reading the connections between the societies of

[10] See for instance the work of Olivier Roy, and in particular his study *Globalized Islam: The Search for a New Ummah,* (New York: Columbia UP, 2004), which focuses on renovating doctrines and behaviors against the background of a lack of culture and sectarian attitudes related to sometimes violent forms of re-Islamization.

emigration and immigration.[11] Death links two families: the members of the families who remained in the "home" country and those who left, which extends family histories beyond the usual systems of alliances and generational successions. If, at the outset, one man leaves alone with the support of his family and group of origin to go seek economic opportunities in another country (with the idea of returning home ultimately abandoned during his lifetime), after two or three generations, a complex system has developed that branches out in time and in each of the two countries concerned. Death takes hold of these two family groups within the continuity of a system of relations, which may have been very well maintained in spite of the distance between them or stretched thin by this separation. The repatriation of a dead person obliges them to reconnect, and it can also serve to repair relations.

The death of the oldest person who was the first to leave is a moment at which everyone reflects on their relationships with these two territories, a moment for counting what has been gained and lost, reflecting on the suffering alleviated by distancing oneself from extreme poverty, as well as on the suffering exacerbated through exile. Informing others of the will to have one's body repatriated to the village of origin can correspond to the will to reunite a family that diasporic situations have scattered, to make the succession of generations visible again—the moment to close a migratory cycle that had been initiated with the idea of going back while the person who migrated was still alive. According to the analysis of Clara Saraiva and José Mapril, This burial in the land of one's ancestors constitutes a celebration of the union with family networks and a victory over the division and separation imposed by daily life.[12] The question of the burial site is first and foremost linked to a family history, even when the inhumation in France is proposed, because of a

[11] That is the initial hypothesis adopted by three researchers for an inquiry carried out in Quebec, who at the same time pointed out the small number of scientific points of reference on the crosses between immigration, mourning, and transnational links. Lilyane Rachédi, Véronique Leduc, and Josiane Legall, " Transnational Networks, Immigrant Families and Mourning," *Lien social et Politiques*, 2010 (64): 175-187.
[12] Clara Saraiva and José Mapril, "The Place of a 'Good Death' for Migrants from Bangladesh and Guinea-Bissau in Portugal," *Revue européenne des migrations internationales,* 2012 (28.3) *La mort en migration.*

link in this case with the living—children and grandchildren—as a way of asserting that the deceased had built a family, of which he will be considered to be the founder. "The most important identity-based question concerning the dead in immigration resides in the imperative of having to choose between the dead and the living."[13] In the second or perhaps third generation, every member of a family or group of siblings can consider for herself the different possibilities in terms of funerary rituals. Deciding to repatriate a close relative or one's own repatriation is the result of a system with constraints, but also, more than is often said, the expression of a freedom of choice, whose meaning can be polymorphous enough to enable us to get around the religious tradition; whereas, a significant part of the motivation can be the recognition of a migratory family history of which one chooses to be the heir, or even of a postcolonial history.

The death of a migrant results in the very strong co-presence of these two models—a moment at which the family that remained in the "home" country takes as a pretext the fragility of the mourning travelers to overplay collective configurations of the extended family, of the circle of neighbors, of the village community, and of the Muslim community, as a demonstration of the "lost values" of those who chose the path of personal emancipation and individuation. Yet this same model also concerns those who decided to remain in the "home" country. Those close to the deceased, who are tired as they get off the airplane, and sometimes defenseless in a country whose codes they do not always completely understand, appreciate the capacity of the family to organize the events with limited means. The possible administrative arrangements highlight the ongoing relationship with the body and their limited

[13] Observation made by Marc Antoine Berthod in his work focusing on death among deceased Puerto Ricans who are repatriated from New York. He also shows that, despite the importance of the debate on Puerto Rican nationalism, it is above all family, economic, and relational factors that influence the decision. Marc Antoine Berthod, « Expérience migratoire et identité dans la mort transnationale: les défunts portoricains rapatriés de New-York », *Canadian Journal of Latin American and Caribbean Studies*, 2006 vol 31 no. 61: 145-168.

room to maneuver with respect to the chains of people involved, who in France maintained those close to the deceased in a role, admittedly one in which they make decisions and accompany the process, but most often distant from the body itself. The intense involvement of the members of the diasporic family, during the three days of funerary rituals in the country of burial, is also a moment for assessing one's distance from and attachments to the culture of the deceased ancestor. The reactions to the different ways of expressing grief (externalization / internalization of sorrow) are often considered to constitute differences that have become irreversible, as are the reinforced gender roles during the funerary rituals linked to the partitioning of space, the division of tasks, and other elements. Finally, most often mentioned in the interviews is how death sheds light on two models of society: one based on a process of individuation, and the other on collective logics. We could make the hypothesis that the suffering linked to mourning tends to exacerbate these positions.

Although other research has insisted on the circulatory phenomena they set in motion,[14] the representations of migratory processes tend to consolidate a two-time model of departure and arrival. In this model, the burial place is considered to be one of the keys for interpreting the integration of immigrants with Maghreb origins in French society,[15] which produces a verification of the link between culture and place. The repatriation of a body corresponds to carrying out one more action in what has become a circulatory culture. If we relate the repatriation of a deceased individual to phenomena concerning the duplication of inhabited spaces (the house in the village that has become a vacation

[14] See for instance the seminal work of Abdelmalek Sayad, who was one of the first scholars to point out the indissociable nature of emigration and immigration, rejecting an immobile sociology in his attempt to comprehend a world in movement. Abdelmalek Sayad, *La Double Absence. Des illusions de l'émigré aux souffrances de l'immigré*, (Paris: Seuil, 1999). Alain Tarrius's research also reveals the logics of circulatory territories, transmigrations, and other forms of migratory societies that exist today sometimes invisibly beyond nation-states, and constitute an argument in favor of an anthropology of movement.

[15] Yassine Chaïb, « Le rapatriement.»

home), the circulation of goods, and access to services (in particular healthcare), and the condensation of space-times linked to new technologies, it would correspond to an ultimate form of transnational practices. Analyzing the repatriations of the deceased within a diasporic cultural perspective can enable a link to be made with the work of *Cultural Studies*, and repatriation can be analyzed as "It is therefore important to see the diasporic perspective on culture as subversive of traditional nation-oriented cultural models. Like other globalizing processes cultural globalization is de-territorializing in its effects."[16] To the notion of post mortem spatial identity proposed by Yassine Chaïb,[17] we propose to link the complex inventions related to repatriations and the emergence of a transnational, transcultural, and modern conscience.

The Deceased, Communities, States

The deceased have also written a page of migratory history in so far as they very quickly constituted a key element in a chain of community-based solidarity organizations. The institutionalization of these organizations, and their links with the countries from which the migrants originated—including financial ones—have continued to consolidate this process, which has had an impact on the choices made by individuals as well as by families. An accidental or premature death could strike the first migrants, who came alone to work in France and of which the repatriation of the body was the only conceivable solution. Very quickly it became a symbol of the necessary solidarity among compatriots: friends collected money at the café or on the construction site. Nobody took the risk of breaking this chain of solidarity, because everyone knew the expenses could not be met by the family back in the "home country," for which an airplane ticket was far too expensive. With the advent of family reunification practices and community-based organizations, associations were established on the basis of national, community, and/or religious criteria, and then progressively in relation to the construction of

[16] See Stuart Hall "Thinking the Diaspora. Home-Thoughts from Abroad," *Small Axe*, (Vol. 3, 1999): 1-18.
[17] Chaïb, « Le repatriement »

mosques and centers for cultural organizations and associations. Yearly dues were established, with a sliding price scale based on age, and people would contribute for themselves as well as their children. The dues collector was a compatriot to whom this money was paid every year. The reminders sent in case of non-payment were a way of reminding people of their reciprocal commitments and links to their community, and it does not seem to be so simple to do away with this chain of solidarity. In addition, because repatriation is paid for in advance, abandoning it when death approaches also seems to be a bad financial choice. Moreover, the very principle of repatriation insurance can commit others to a decision about which they cannot even express their own opinion, since many parents pay dues for their children, which encroaches upon their future desires. Companies have specialized in repatriation and run sites that provide all the information needed. They are fully operational funeral insurance companies with activities for specific destinations, including the Maghreb, Africa, and Turkey. For example, the DITIB manages funeral funds for the religious funeral ceremonies of its members and the repatriation of bodies to Turkey. This network has activities throughout Europe and for the diaspora represents the Turkish-Islamic Union for Religious Affairs, which is directly linked to the Turkish Prime Minister. The countries of origin of the living migrants act to retrieve the deceased members of their diaspora. Since its independence, the Tunisian state has paid for the repatriation of all Tunisians living abroad; the repatriation of these dead bodies has never been challenged, even during the revolution. Following this model, the Algerian State decided to cover the costs of repatriating the mortal remains of Algerian nationals who live abroad. Officially adopted by the government in accordance with Article 136 of the 2015 Finance Law, this law went into effect in January 2017. On both sides of the border, in relation to the places of inhumation, we can read a conception of the Nation linked to its soil. The countries of emigration encourage the repatriation of those participating in their diasporas, in an ultimate effort to renationalize their dead bodies. In France, the 2008 circular sent by the Ministry of the Interior to prefects and mayors, which encourages faith-based organizations, is a gesture made to better accompany the integration of immigrant populations. In its capacity as a host country, France defends the idea of a "living community of the deceased, that is, a Nation that includes in its territory all living and deceased individuals.[18] This objective reinforces the idea of the definitive choice that the migrant or French person of foreign descent must make to earn their place in the Nation. It is the model of the Western nation-state, based on the (generally implicit) presupposition of cultural homogeneity, even if the creation of confessional circles would tend to make visible a multicultural society. Yet the creation of circles, if it seems to be related to the acceptance of building a common life, while at the same time marking differences, also seems to be accepted as only a (necessary) moment in a history, because the end of mass immigration and the temporal limits of burial plots do not accommodate this singularity in death in the long term.[19]

The acknowledgement of funerary rituals in terms of social justice and immigrant citizenship rights can never be simply a matter of transferring financial means from the host country to the country of origin, nor of facilitating the trip to France of family members who remained in the home country (by issuing visas for them). In his research on Congolese migrants in Canada,[20] Mambo Tabu Masinda argues that the non-recognition of the funerary rituals of immigrants constitutes a violation of their citizenship rights, which opens new lines of inquiry about what could be a new logic for multicultural policies: to effect a radical reconfiguration of the particular and the universal, of liberty and equality with difference."[21]

[18] Arnaud Esquerre, *Les os, les cendres et l'Etat.*

[19] Jordi Moreras and Sol Tarrès have shown that the administration of funerary diversity in Spain makes Muslim cemeteries places of alterity. Jordi Moreras and Sol Tarrès, « Les cimetières musulmans en Espagne: des lieux d'altérité » in *Revue européenne des migrations internationales,* 28, no. 3 (2012).

[20] Mambo Tabu Masinda, « Citoyenneté et rituels funéraires des immigrants. Le cas de migrants congolais au Canada, » *Revue européenne des migrations internationales*, 30, no. 3 and 4 (2014), http://remi.revues.org/6997.

[21] Stuart Hall, "The Multi-cultural Question," *Un/Settled Multiculturalisms. Diasporas, Entanglement, Transruptions*, Barnor Hesse (ed.) (London: Zed Books, 2000), 209-241.

An Inquiry Brought to the Stage

Western theater has been essentially organized around a vocalized written text. As Michel de Certeau argues, speech usually constitutes an exteriority or what remains vis-à-vis writing.[22] Our inquiry work gave people who are usually deprived of speech the chance to speak, but the deciphering work that consists in writing the voice, made the spoken word disappear. One of the challenges in transforming a written text into a theatrical production is to re-establish its oral and corporeal status, and also a co-presence. In the experience we describe, the research was conducted before the theater project and was continued in the writing process, as well as in the different steps in the staging work. This play is not akin—in either its subject matter or form—to militant theater, as it can be used by employees to save their jobs or by authors who take up their struggles.[23] It transmits knowledge, aims to make people understand, while fully accepting its civic dimension. In addition to the meaning of the text and the questioning conveyed by the narratives, we see the progression and the trials and errors of the researchers as they attempt to draw the audience into the inquiry without imposing definitive scientific results, suggesting instead possibilities and allowing the audience to interpret what they see. The time of the inquiry is one during which we follow the current of meaning, let ourselves be transported by it; it is the instant in which our feelings are amplified, exaggerated, and migrate toward the public space in search of eyewitnesses. It is in the current of meaning that convictions are shared and memory is solicited.[24] This reflexive process can be read as a political reactivation of public space.

[22]Michel de Certeau, *The Practice of Everyday Life*, trans. Steven Rendall (Berkeley: University of California Press,1988).

[23] Such is the case of *501 blues*—a play whose staged version directed by Christophe Martin was written from material produced in creative writing classes, and then played by the workers whose struggle it recounts; *Daewoo*, a novel by François Bon (Paris: Fayard, 2004), and a play directed by Charles Tordjman, which tell the story of the shutdown of the Daewoo factory in Villers-La-Montagne, based on an abundant corpus of sociological materials including eye-witness accounts, facts, and figures.

[24] Jean-François Laé, Numa Murard, « L'enquête, l'enquêteur et la perception, » Les *Récits du malheur,* (Paris: *Descartes et Cie,* 1995)*,* 169-170.

The play unfolds in a succession of situations, like a patchwork whose overall plot is defined by scientific issues. It is based on two movements: the first aims to show how different scales are interconnected, and to explore the questions of death and repatriation in light of the evolutions of globalized societies (beyond the Muslim world); the second seeks to blend the intimate with the political by focusing on the body of the deceased in all its dimensions. Having a grasp of this overall process, sketched out in its scientific dimensions, influenced how this play was written and staged. Once the order of the main texts had been found, the theatrical requirements pointed to all of the interstices and transitions that had to be invented. Theater's specific constraints and mechanisms imposed their limitations on the writing, but were resources as well. In theater, meaning is manufactured through the power of orality and images. A great amount of work went into clarifying the writing, avoiding enumerations, simplifying the vocabulary, and eliminating any comments, which have more to do with the actors' interpretation than how they say the text. The vocalized text is short when we compare it to the amount of room available on the page; bodies, their movements, moments of silence, and variations of the voices reinvent a movement that begins in the text and goes beyond it: "theater (...) inhabited and penetrated by a powerful urge, of writing in *acts*, with no words or between words, in the interstices of their respiration, in the space between them or in their enjambment." [25]

At the heart of the theatrical experience, there is of course its collective singularity, its reception always occurs in the presence of others, and if this effect of co-presence influences its reception, it is never superior to the force of the spectator's solitude: In a theatre [...] there are only ever individuals who plot their own paths in the forest of things [...]. The combined power of the spectators does not stem from their belonging to a collective body or some specific form of interactivity.

[25] Laurent Mauvignier in *Visages d'un récit,* (Nantes: Capricci, 2015), 19. This essay relates variations that concern a piece of fiction, in an attempt to understand the process unfolding in the shifts from one form to another: an unfinished scenario: *Tout mon amour* transformed into a play, which then comes back to cinema.

It is the power each of them has to translate what she perceives in her own way, to link it to the unique intellectual adventure that makes it similar to all others, when in fact this adventure does not resemble any other.[26] Jacques Rancière recognizes in the power to associate and dissociate, and to link what we know with what we ignore, the possible emancipation of the spectator of theater.

Core Issues in the play Following the Dead

Through the issue of repatriation, all of the spectators are invited to partake in a kind of decentering of culture, in relation to practices and representations that are specific to each group, even if death also seems to be a subject conducive to making people more open to alterities, because opinions and beliefs are so fragile at these destabilizing moments. The moment and situation of theater make it possible, then, to cross over some personal boundaries, to help us understand and approach others in a decentering process, and to hear what they can teach us about the world we share. Becoming conscious of the freedom of choice as regards funerary rituals and related issues, which are revealed by the cultural, ecological, and political facets of the play, hint at the possible appropriation of a field previously off limits, of a decidedly unthinkable domain of thought. May the play *Following the Dead* take up one of the avenues of inquiry opened by Michel de Certeau, when he writes The impossibility of expressing death is inscribed in all of the procedures that hem in death or drive it beyond the limits of the city, beyond time, work, and language, so as to shield a place. [...] *the place where I am not.*[27] Ultimately, *thinking from the borde*r embodies this issue, not to update our knowledge about the divisions and separations of different forms of knowledge and representation, rather to find places where we can go beyond them.

[26] Jacques Rancière, *The Emancipated Spectator,* trans. Gregory Elliott (London, New York: Verso, 2009), 16-17 (my adaptation).
[27] Michel de Certeau, *The Practice of Everyday Life,* Chapter 14, "The Unnamable," 194.

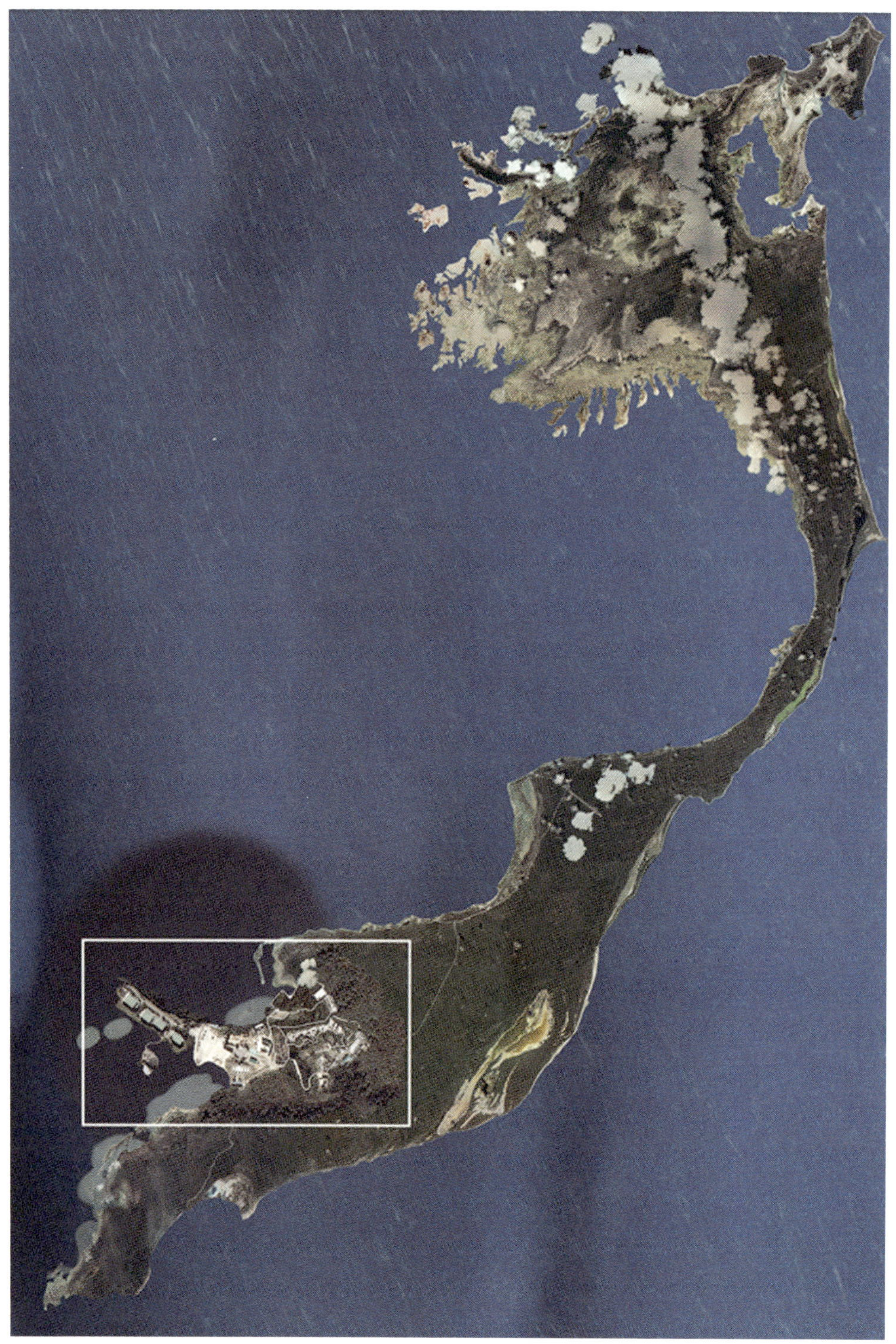

THE INVENTION OF THE NORTH: A NEW TYPOLOGY

> "I see what I believe"
> Theodore Roethke

The Invention of the North: A New Typology is a multimedia platform that aims to articulate the contradictory narratives *by* and *about* the North (North Korea), based on the borderin this case the DMZ, or demilitarized zone—which is taken both as a subject of my study and as a method. At the origin of my interest in the border, as it appears in this project, lies the process through which asylum applications are examined in France. On the one hand, this procedure is supposed to establish the *legitimacy* of the requests vis-à-vis the Geneva Convention; on the other, based on the *credibility* of the testimony according to the subjective and discretionary judgement of the examiners, who when making their judgements, find themselves both in the order of law and in the order of beliefs. Whereas the order of law has relatively well-defined textual sources, the order of beliefs is based on criteria linked to the assessment of the *circumstantial* and *personalized* quality of the testimony, which varies considerably according to the examiners and how they defend their*personal convictions.*[1]

An echo of this relationship between the order of law and the order of beliefs can be heard in the DMZ, the border between the two Koreas. In her book *DMZ Crossing: Performing Emotional Citizenship Along the Korean Border*[2], Suk-Young Kim describes the double affiliation of a Korean citizen to the North and to the South: a constitutional affiliation, in the form of systematic political opposition to the other Korea, and an emotional affiliation linked to the nostalgia for a unified Korea.

[1] The question of the *truthfulness* of the testimony is another story. Here, it is only a question of appearances as they are linked to the quality of the narrative, which we find in the narratives *by* and *about* the North: I have already defined the construction of this narrative as *fiction expressed in a single voice*, of which we will find an example further below, in the Orientalist construction of the West in narratives about the North.

[2] New York: Columbia University Press, 2014.

Christiane Carlut, *Fallen from the Sky*, January 2018.
From the site "http://christiane-carlut.fr/Linventiondunord/0-index.html" @courtesy of the artist.

My interest in the DMZ, an extremely curious border object, was reinforced by the enigma represented by the Democratic People's Republic of Korea (North Korea) to Westerners. My research was based on the gathering of information, mainly theoretical, historical, and geopolitical essays, but also on reports from the voyages of writers, artists, journalists, and even tourists who traveled to the North, and gave their accounts of it in blogs, essays, photos, and films—sometimes shaped by their attachments to their own biases. Finally, my six trips in the DMZ, four from the South, and two from the North, enabled me to clarify, flesh out a bit, confirm, or contradict the information gathered. I discovered an amazingly diverse body of stories, with the greatest scientific rigor or the most worn-out stereotypes, establishing knowledge and experiences that were impossible to reconcile or even to articulate, due to the extreme contradictions expressed in them. The difficulty of giving form to this gigantic ensemble seemed to be insurmountable, unless I chose to start with the form of the border itself—conflict, confrontation, and contradiction—, and transform it into a non-linear form, which would ultimately lead me to build a multimedia platform. Certain particular fields of interest contributed substantially to informing my research workand the very construction of the site, including Orientalism, our relationships to History, the notion of heterotopy, and my interest in the questions raised through the articulation of factuality and fiction.

Orientalisms

One of Edward Said's motivations for writing *Orientalism*[3] was the Western media coverage of the 1973 Arab-Israeli War: presented as cowardly, the Arabs were always said to have been defeated. Clichés and stereotypes constitute the recurrent weapons of the political issues that circulate in the news from one side of the border to the other, and the media, as Alain Gresh writes in other circumstances

[3] New York: Pantheon Books, 1978.

"has stopped taking interest in the actual country itself (its political and social life), and instead only focuses on caricatures."[4] In her article *"North Korea, the Country that Arouses Unlimited Media Fantasies,"* the journalist Charlotte Boitiaux writes: "Fascinated by the North Korean dictatorship, the Western media has increasingly given in to the temptation to relay the most extravagant rumors about the Pyongyang regime. Often even going so far as to not verify information."[5]

Numerous examples offer proof of this attitude: the execution, announced by Han Ki-beom, the deputy director of South Korea's National Intelligence Service (NIS), of the defense minister Hyon Yong-chol, reportedly executed "by a ZPU-4 anti-aircraft gun at a firing range in the presence of several hundred onlookers[...] for having fallen asleep during an official parade."[6] Chang Song-taek, Kim Jong-un's uncle-in-law, condemned to death for having "betrayed the nation" was reportedly devoured alive on December 12, 2013 by a pack of 120 famished dogs. Meanwhile, ABC News reported the existence of an "invisible mobile phone," used by Kim Jong-un to help coach the North Korean soccer team from afar during a game.[7] The satirical news site *Gorafi* laid it on unreasonably thick in its 2014 show: "To prevent exiles, Kim Jong-un installs a giant strip of flypaper along its border [...] with China, Russia, and South Korea."[8] Articles published in China in the guise of jokes are republished in South Korean and US newspapers as serious news. All of these Orientalisms standardize and impoverish our visions of the country in ways that facilitate and organize the manipulation of it, to "enlighten" what people see according to the

---

[4] About Iran, see: http://blog.mondediplo.net/2013-06-16-Iran-un-echec-pour-le-Guide-et-pour-la-presse, Monday June 17, 2013.

[5] http://www.france24.com/fr/20150515-coree-nord-rumeurs-fantasmes-kim-jong-un-medias-informations-cruaute-executions.

[6] Le Parisien, May 2015: http://www.leparisien.fr/international/coree-du-nord-un-ministre-execute-au-canon-anti-aerien-pour-deloyaute-13-05-2015-4767537.php.

[7] http://abcnews.go.com/International/world-cup-2010-north-korean-coach-talks-kim/story?id=10931655.

[8] http://www.legorafi.fr/2014/05/05/pour-empecher-les-exils/.

interests at stake.[9] North Korea remains a product of Orientalism, the Western discourse on the Orient, this "Western style for dominating, restructuring, and having authority over the Orient."[10] The Orient, which Western culture according to Edward Said, took to be an inferior and repressed form of itself. Already in 1904, Jack London himself expressed in his reports his admiration for colonial Japan and its racist biases with regard to Koreans: "[The Korean] is certainly the most inefficient of human creatures, lacking all initiative and achievement, and the only thing in which he shines is the carrying of burdens on his back. As a draught animal and packhorse he is a success."[11] The invisibility of Brian Myers's sources in *La race des purs: Comment les Nord-Coréens se voient,*[12] contrasts with the omnipresent condescending or even racist orientalist clichés he piles on the North Koreans, and with his arrogant judgements. We can observe, still today, how much the construction of the Orient—here of North Korea—is inscribed within a relationship of power and Occidental domination of the Orient. A significant body of historical and pseudo-historical literature offers its readers a remarkable range of prejudices and stereotypes, which are never based on what can be found in historical archives, and are due to what Siegfried Kracauer called a state of (mental) paralysis.[13]

The Relationship to History

My website maintains a relationship vis-à-vis history that is close to what Ivan Jablonca calls a methodological fiction,"[14] which enables questions to be asked about history by means of fiction, taking

[9] "to be a European or American [...] is by no means an inert fact. It meant and means being aware, however dimly, that one belongs to a power with definite interests in the Orient." Edward Said, *Orientalism*, 11.

[10] Said, 3.

[11] "Royal Road a Sea of Mud," in King Hendricks and Irving Shepherd, eds., *Jack London Reports* (Garden City NY: Doubleday & Co., 1970), 44.

[12] Paris: Saint-Simon, 2011.

[13] *From Caligari to Hitler: A Psychological History of the German Film*, (Princeton: Princeton UP, 2019).[14] *De Caligari à Hitler : Une histoire psychologique du cinéma allemand*, Ed. l'Âge d'Homme, 2009.

[14] *L'histoire est une littérature contemporaine-Manifeste pour les sciences sociales*, (Paris: Seuil, La librairie du XXIe siècle, 2014).

distance voluntarily from the real in an attempt to understand it. The role of fiction in my site, whether visual or textual, is to stage conflicts between documentary elements. The story focuses on a specific part of the world, the DMZ, the two Koreas, and interpretations that are so contradictory according to the sources (North or South Korea, the United States, Europe, or another part of the world), such that the staging of these contradictions can only be useful for history itself: for exposing the conflicts in the thoughts about the conflict, and giving form to it is yet another way of making history.

In a famous book, published in 1997, *A Thousand Years of Nonlinear History*, writes le peuple qui manque, the philosopher Manuel De Landa argues that we should no longer consider history as a chain of events linking causes and effects, but rather made up of reversals and bifurcations.[15] That is precisely how the issues on my site were embodied, a mapping of the investigative processes shaping the narratives and forms of these reversals and bifurcations of the border, a veritable Borges-like "garden of forking paths"[16] in time and space, history and geography, where multiple visible and invisible interests cross, as well as multiple levels of approaches and fields. This mapping is an attempt to not let the simplistic clichés (military, political, media) act alone, but instead to lead website visitors toward places, narratives, and images that put them into perspective, or even short-circuit them.

The action in one of the scenarios on my website, *The Partition*, takes place in an imaginary cinema studioa blend of those in the North and those in the South—, where visitors wait when they arrive on the site. A man and a woman live and work in this studio, maintain, and repair the scenery, and pass without seeing each other. The other protagonists include an itinerant theater troupe, an amnesiac French soldier, who is a survivor of the Korean War, a doe, chased by a stray

[15] At their presentation of the event *One Thousand Years of Nonlinear History.* See: https://www.facebook.com/peuplequimanque.
[16] Borges, *Fictions*, 1944.

dog from one side of the border to the other, which is itself chased by the theater troupe. The scenes in which the man figures are shot in South Korean cinema studios, and those featuring the woman in North Korean studios. The fiction becomes a space of reunification through the editing. The fictional porosity of the border, and the relationship between the dreamed, past, and future times of Korean unity constitute the mechanism that creates the "infinite"[17] present of the scenario.

On the other side of these fictional relationships with history, historians such as the American Bruce Cumings and the Russian Andreï Lankov, as well as the ex-American soldier, lawyer, and activist-pacifist Brian Willson, through his articles on the military history of the United States, make enlightened comments about Korean history by actively consulting archives, and overturning the stereotypes about Korean war history. The Korean War, which gave birth to and established the shape of the DMZ, remains in France a territory of investigation beyond the scope of our general knowledge, in spite of the fact that France sent troops there, albeit under the military authority of Americans and thus according to their objectives.[18] The North Koreans were stigmatized by these ideological orientations of history, and few voices have been raised to try to rectify them. One of the motivations of my site is to re-establish these points of view, and to make them accessible.

Brian Willson[19] describes the installation of the future far right-wing dictator Sygman Rhee by the Americans in South Korea in 1945. Rhee subsequently put in place powerful paramilitary groups that worked with the official U.S. security and intelligence forces, and organized the systematic purge of democratically elected opposition forces. From August 15, 1945 to June 30, 1949, during their "legal

[17] "that the present is indefinite, that the future has no reality other than as a present hope, that the past has no reality other than as a present memory" Borges, *Fictions*, 1944.
[18] Erwann Bergott, *Bataillon de Corée-Les volontaires français 1950-1953*, (Paris: Presses de la Cité, 1984).
[19] "Brief History US of Korean Peace and Reunification," 2013, http://www.brianwillson.com/brief-history-us-sabotage-of-korean-peace-and-reunification/.

occupation," the American armed forces looked the other way as a genocide was being committed that killed about 500,000 people.[20] On March 31, 1952, the Report on U.S. Crimes in Korea by the Commission of the International Association of Democratic Lawyers established the utilization by the United States of bacteriological and chemical weapons and the assassination of 2,500,000 civilians, which has been defined as a "genocide" by the American historian Bruce Cumings.[21]

> According to Cumings, during the Korean War (1950-53), there was: Continuous large-scale dropping, by Americans of incendiary bombs with napalm on North Korea, and then, in the final phase of the war, threats to use nuclear and chemical weapons. These facts are, however, quite unknown, even to historians, and the analyses in the mainstream media concerning nuclear issues in North Korea over the last ten years have never mentioned them.[22]

In 2000, the South Korea Truth and Reconciliation Commission, whose role was to investigate this question before and during the Korean war, reported that:

> Ultimately, it appears that after the war began in June [1950], South Korean authorities and auxiliary right-wing youth squads executed around 100,000 people and dumped them into trenches and mines, or simply threw them into the sea. (...) The North Koreans and their allies killed hundreds in Seoul (...), and others towns, totaling more than 1,100 (...). However, much as it may discomfit American sensibilities, the record shows that Communists atrocities constituted about one sixth of the total number of cases, and tended to be more discriminating.[23]

The Sinchon Museum of American War Atrocities, which is in North Korea, bears witness to this history, but the atrocities are

---

[20] The lowest estimate is 100,000 and the highest is 800,000 people killed.
[21] *The Korean War: A History*, (New York: Modern Library Chronicles, 2011.
[22] Le Monde diplomatique, December 2004, translation Christiane Carlut.
[23] Cumings, *The Korean War: A History*, 202.

attributed to the American military forces rather than to the Koreans themselves. Very few international visitors go to this museum.These historical data help us understand much better the extremely tense relations that still exist between the North and the South, and the latter's ally, the United States. Here, I must remind readers that the military agreements between the United States and South Korea stipulate that if the North were to attack the South, Americans would be in charge of the military operations in the South. In fact, this is more or less what they give the impression of doing in the DMZ. North Korea, concludes Bruce Cumings in his article When the United States Destroys a Country to Save It,[24] has not endeavored to equip itself with weapons of mass destruction for no reason: The United States is the only world power that has used the atomic bomb, and its policy of dissuasion is based on the threat of using such weapons again in Korea."

According to Rüdiger Frank, professor of East Asian Economy and Society at the University of Vienna, three events convinced Pyongyang to develop nuclear weapons.[25] First, Gorbachevs decision to put an end to the arms race, because the West, instead of helping the Russian economy, destroyed its empire one country at a time. This included the total annihilation of Saddam Husseins Iraq following the concessions made to Western countries, Gaddafi abandoning his programs to develop weapons of mass destruction, and ultimately being assassinated in 2011. Stephen Gowan, a Canadian writer and activist made the following analysis of these events:

> After the US/UK invasion of Iraq in March 2003, North Korea's foreign ministry declared that 'the Iraqi war shows that to allow disarmament through inspections does not help avert a war, but rather sparks it,' Gowan concludes that "only a tremendous

---

[24] Bruce Cumings, "Quand les Etats-Unis détruisaient un pays pour le sauver, Mémoires de feu en Corée du Nord," Le Monde diplomatique, December 2004, p. 22-23.
[25] Stephan Gowan: https://gowans.wordpress.com/2016/03/06/why-un-sanctions-against-north-korea-are-wrong/.

military deterrent force can prevent attacks on states the US dislikes."[26]

All of these documents, these heterogeneous relationships to history, can be found on my site, ready for battle, standing up against each other: fictional accounts, stereotypes and clichés, and historical narratives, which illustrate the geopolitical and historical complexity of the construction of the DMZ and of North Korea. Michel de Certeau would say that "poaching" strategies are at play, combining major and minor modes in the restitution of contradictions, "loose associations like those of Ryan Gander, light moments in the sea of constraints... Let hybrid forms act on the division of ideas.

Border Forms

Since its creation in 1953, the conflicts near the border have affected its form, and observing these transformations enabled me to define the form and the methodology of this project. In 1950, the South and the North of Korea were preparing, each on its own side, to invade the other. The North acted more rapidly, and on June 25, 1950, it crossed the border.[27] The Korean War started, and from 1950 to 1953, four million people would be killed or disappear. The Demilitarized Zone (DMZ) has served as a buffer zone between the two Koreas since the end of the war. Paradoxically, whereas there should not be any soldiers or weapons there, it is the most heavily militarized border in the world: in the southern part, there are 650,000 Korean and 28,000 American soldiers along this strip that is 248 kilometers long and 4 kilometers wide. In the northern part, the number is a defense secret," but military experts estimate that the two Koreas have 60% to 70% of their armies on the border, and North Korea has one million soldiers. Officially, the war is not overa simple cease fire has been in force since 1953, and no peace treaty has ever been signed.

[26] Gowan, https://gowans.wordpress.com/2016/03/06/why-un-sanctions-against-north-korea-are-wrong/.

[27] Cumings, *The Korean War: A History*.

This information enables us to better understand the geopolitical stakes and the effects stemming from the pressure felt on both sides of this border, which is not one. Cumings describes it as anon-border of an unfinished war. The war zone of the two Koreas, which has not changed in 64 years, is perhaps what makes Chris Marker say: When a country is divided in two parts by an artificial border, and on both sides abounds the most irreconcilable propaganda, it is naïve to wonder where the war originated: this very border itself is the war.[28] War, as a border form, encourages my *Invention of the North* website to take on the form of open conflict.

The Two fold Affiliation of a Korean Citizen (North/South)

As of the preliminary phase during which archival information about the DMZ was being gathered, a specific, self-legitimizing principle of opposition became strikingly apparent: the two nation-states concerned, North Korea and South Korea, established their respective legitimacies on a *sui generis* system of division, of opposition to the other, in order to, as Peter Andreas says in another context, "symbolically reaffirm[ing] the state's territorial authority."[29] Citizenship, on both sides of the DMZ, is based on this strong idea: "People's affiliation to the state is defined not by what they support but by what they oppose."[30]

The oxymoron brother enemy is often used to refer to people who are on the other side of the border. It expresses the full magnitude of the historical ambivalence that has constituted this part of the world, which has not been modified by the end of the cold war. On the one hand, the hatred of the government of the other side, which is carefully maintained by the leaders of both countries, against

[28] Philippe Pons, *Corée du nord, un état-guérilla en mutation*, (Paris: Gallimard, 2016), 14.

[29] About the Mexican border. Peter Andreas, *Border Games: Policing the U.S.-Mexico Divide*, (Ithaca: Cornell University Press, 2001).

[30] Suk-Young Kim: *DMZ crossing: Performing Emotional Citizenship along the Korean Border*, (New York: Colombia University Press, 2014), 6.

the backdrop of the geopolitical and economic strategies of their allies; on the other, the nostalgia of each of the two peoples with regard to the original unity of Korea—this emotional dimension referring to the continually postponed project of *reunification*. Under such circumstances, emotional ties that develop in a community of people who share historical and cultural affinities and cohesion lose their grounding in the formation of citizenship."[31]

A Korean citizen is thus painfully constituted through a double affiliation: first, constitutional, based on the political division (a good citizen, in the North or in the South, is a citizen that is opposed to the other Korea); second, emotional, based on their territorially united origins, divided family, and desired destiny—reunification. The aging of Korean citizens who are separated by the (American) border,[32] has resulted in the progressive forgetting of their family members isolated on the other side of the DMZ. All that remains is the nostalgia for a united history that keeps alive the dream of a common future with a pacified history. The constitutional reason divides in the present, while individual and collective emotions unite, via the past and the future, via nostalgia and hope.

This radical exclusion, by means of citizenship, of Koreans on the other side, also has linguistic repercussions. Since the partition of Korea, the Korean language has become split, in the North and South, in terms of the pronunciation, writing, grammar, vocabulary, and accent. This exclusion has taken on the form of a will for complete appropriation, all the way to the very name(s) of Korea, to the very existence of a common term for referring to the country:

There is no simple term in Korean for expressing Korea" so much (that we use) the word K'oria (the simple transcription of the

[31] Kim.

[32] The division of Korea is the result of a line drawn on the 38th parallel by two U.S. military officers, Dean Rusk and Charles Bonesteel, on August 10, 1945, which was determined by the will of the United States to maintain the capital, Seoul, under its control. This military process excluded the Koreans themselves from the very decisions that established the division of their country. Cumings, *Korean War,* 103.

English Korea) to express [it] [...] We are confronted with, no longer two, but at least four Koreas, according to where we find ourselves, for referring to it.[33]

For example, in North Korean, North Korea calls itself *Chosŏn*, and calls South Korea, *Nam Chosŏn*, the *Chosŏn of the South*. In South Korean, South Korea is *Han'guk,* while North Korea is *Pukhan*, the *North of South Korea*. This linguistic multiplication of Korea is reflected in the almost never absolute and often relativistic terms employed to refer to the territories on my website.

Meta-border

In the words of Valérie Gelézeau, the DMZ constitutes:

a good example of what the geographer Michel Fouchet calls a meta-border; that is, a border that temporally and spatially goes beyond the territory in which it was originally traced. [...] The inter-Korean border has been exported [...] to Kazakhstan, where the (diasporic) Russophone Korean community was the focus of a veritable language war waged by the two Korean states at the turn of the 1990s [...] to teach these communities the true" Korean language.[34]

The 1978 kidnapping by Kim Jong-il of Shin Sang-ok, a star filmmaker in South Korea, and of his wife, the actress Choi Eun-hee, who were "invited" by the Leader to renew North Korean cinema, also falls within the scope of this meta-border. The Silmido island episode also externalized the line: in 1968, a group of 31 North Korean soldiers infiltrated South Korea to assassinate President Park Chung-hee, but was stopped before achieving its mission. In response, the Korean Central Inteligence Agency (KCIA) decided to send a group of petty criminals, Unit 684, to assassinate Kim Il-sung. However, the

[33] Valérie Gelézeau, Schizo-coréanologies. De la frontière spatiale aux discours de la division. Aspects et tendances de la culture coréenne contemporaine, June 2014, Nantes, France, <halshs-01140555>

[34] Gelézeau, 7.

presidential elections brought a period of détente between the North and the South, and the KCIA decided to eliminate Unit 684.

As Etienne Balibar has written: "Some borders are no longer at all located at borders, but are omnipresent elsewhere, everywhere selective controls are enforced."[35] The border has extended in North Korea, in which invisible borders abound: people cannot travel from one city to another without authorization,and there are checkpoints throughout the country. The specific form of my site, with its dead ends, obstacles, checkpoints, and even pure and simple expulsions corresponds to these mobile and ramified aspects of the border. Not to mention the Border-Being…

The Border in Motion and under Construction Remains Unfinished

In Schizo-coréanologies. De la frontière spatiale aux discours de la division,[36] Valérie Gelézeau evokes a border in motion, which is always under construction and unfinished, in contradiction with the image conveyed by the media of a fossil of the Cold War. Between 1945 and 1950, territories went from the South to the North and conversely, and the front line, after the beginning of the Korean War in 1950, continued to shift the limits of the territory. In the border zone (in the broad sense of the term), the zones in which there are restrictions on the movements of the civilian population that lives near the border (such as the Civilian Control Zone) were also reduced in size at the beginning of the 1980s to make the lives of inhabitants easier." In addition, the two Koreas never negotiated the limits of their territorial waters, and the famous Northern Limit Line is in reality the border that was established *de facto* by the UN and South Korea after the war, but it has never been acknowledged by North Korea.

The regular naval battles in this zone (1999, 2002, 2009) [...], the sinking of the South Korean corvette, the Ch'ŏnan, in March 2010 [...] and the bombing of the South Korean island of Yŏnp'yŏng in

[35] Etienne Balibar, *La crainte des masses*, (Paris: éditions Galilée, 1997).
[36] https://halshs.archives-ouvertes.fr/halshs-01140555, June 2014, Nantes.

November 2010 are the concrete expressions of the territorial conflicts that characterize this border still under construction.[37]

Governmental changes in the South have had major effects on the form of the border. 1998 to 2008 was a period of openness in the framework of the Sunshine Policy implemented by President Kim Dae-jung, also known as the "South Korea's engagement policy toward North Korea." From an economic point of view, joint projects were developed, with notably the creation of special economic zones in Kaesŏng and Kŭmgang. From an emotional point of view, families in the North and South were able to meet at the border line: Valérie Gelézeau writes that "During this period, crossing the border took on major imaginary and symbolic significance in both countries." In South Korea, at the Dorasan train station, we can still read today: "Not the last station from the South, but the first station toward the North!" After a few years of détente, the South Korean policy started leaning strongly to the right again, and turned off the Sunshine Policy, which has perhaps just been reawakened in light of the recent presidential elections.

Forms of My Site

My study of border forms for *The Invention of the North* website, required me to adopt specific forms and points of view. The most striking examples of them are contradiction, conflict, division, exclusion, ambivalence, and the opposition between the (supposedly) rational nature (political and military reason) and the emotional nature of the relationship to the Other Korea. My goal was to get closer to irreconcilable political facts and feelings, opposite interpretations of events, and to the vast expanse of contradictory feelings to leave them a place where they could exist without trying to resolve them. I wanted to attempt to escape from the ideological/media-based

---

[37] Gelézeau, 7.

smoothing operations, from the ones rooted in simplifications and data unification, which impoverish and corrupt data, and lead straight to the formulation and persistence—of stereotypes.

Visitors enter *The Invention of the North* website through space, which places them in the position of an extraterrestrial arriving on Earth. They hover above a forest near the sea, which ends in a peninsula. This imaginary territory is the fruit of the juxtaposition of satellite images from two cinema studios, the *Korean Film Studios*, in Pyongyang, and the *Kofic Namyangju Studios*, west of Seoul, and it situates the site directly in the fictional and phantasmal dimensions of the border. The studios have a common site, a *Choseon* village,[38] which serves as a border and a passage, and is a reference to when Korea was unified. Hovering over this unknown territory, visitors must decide where to land on the ground, in total ignorance of what to expect, and with no points of reference. Their exploration after having landed will continue to be haphazard: many parts are not directly visible, and only appear when the cursor hovers over them. The rules that determine how visitors can navigate on the site must be deduced from experience.

The Invention of the North offers visitors different observation points at which they can start their exploration of various territories, through opposing logics and forms of knowledge, with no mediator or guide. They must compare, organize, and interpret conflicting data, give themselves over to highly diverse and complex points of view, and rebuild the North starting at its border.

As in any tourist agency, there are two ways to visit the site: in "guided" mode, and in a more open, "individually customizable" mode, depending on the point of entry. In the former mode, you can visit the North within the closed space of nine categories: three main

[38] *Choseon* is the historical period during which Korea was governed by the Yi dynasty, which occupied the throne from 1392 to 1910. Each of the two film studios, in North and South Korea, made a reconstruction of a Choseon village.

categories (political-biography, mythobiography, and cinematography), which are subdivided into nine subcategories: The Leader, the People, and the Territory, the Father, the Children, Play Areas, the Filmmaker, the Actors, and the Scenery. These different points of entry condition and limit the access at the border to the North, and demonstrate the extent of a particular relationship to the history of the DMZ and of the DPRK, inscribed between the real and fiction, and which include factual and scientific data, but also purely mythobiographic and cinematographic inventions of the North as well as of the South. The "customizable" mode of visiting the site is paradoxically included in the "guided" mode, and the visitors, who are unaware of this fact, maintain the illusion of roaming around this territory as they please. However, in this mode, they do not have access to all of the different parts of the territory.

The territory is, then, hyper-organized, on the one hand, yet unstructured, on the other. The information communicated may be hierarchically ordered or not, rational or irrational (fanciful, fantastic, fantasist), emotional... Some information does not change, while other information varies, and changes according to when it is accessed. The territory itself is unstable: some parts, in the middle of the ocean, are affected by the tide and disappear or emerge according to the time of the visit. Islets appear suddenly, where visitors can enter at certain times of the day or night, and be able to access elements to which they will not have access the following day. The Yodok penal labor colony No.15, whose existence was denied by North Korean authorities, and which is only visible from the sky via satellite images satellites, is one of these islets that emerge from nowhere, like Silmido, Jejudo, and Tiger and Rabbit Island.

When they enter the site, visitors can take: a) paths that are linear and nonlinear, straight or forking, avenues, streets, trails, trenches, tunnels, and hallways. They may pass through: b) doors, gates, des barricades, roadblocks, checkpoints, and toll gates, and cross: c) bridges, fords, and stairways, but also walls,[39] secret and spatial-temporal passageways, and underground or aerial tunnels. To travel, they may use: d) elevators, moving walkways, bicycles, cars, drones, hovercrafts, and tanks, and observe the scene: e) from afar, close-up, above, below, and the side. Finally, they may chance upon: f) ports, channels, passes, narrow passes, dykes, dead ends, enclaves, and visual or sound obstacles. The "return" function enables visitors to go back to the previous page, or to be jettisoned into an unexpected place, or simply ejected from the site. The site is not a video game, but sometimes flirts with its practices.

The *Border-Being* (the Leader represented in the form of a banner borrowed from Goya[40]), embodies the mobile border, the Meta-border that comes out of nowhere. It can either confine visitors on the page, thus preventing them from leaving it, and suspending their navigation, or it can eject them from the site. The *Border-Being* creates tension between competing logics and conflicting worlds: it is a *space* of fictionalization of the self, of desubjectivation of the other, and taking control, of submission by the other to the extremely hierarchical ordering of powers. It is the embodiment of a radical disidentification of the other in the very drive that characterizes the will to achieve the absolute identification of oneself. It perpetuates discrimination against others and their lack of rights, sequesters speech, and reduces others to silence. It is confronted with indifferentiation and indifference, and has a life hanging in suspense, a life hanging in suspense for its own life (Balibar). It is a hodgepodge mixture (*Borderline*) of the self and of an Other, without knowing if we are ourselves or an Other, or perhaps both at the same time. The Other is a *Shadow Beast* (Gloria Anzaldua): Power clings to it in the hope of gaining access to light, the People bides its time there because shade offers protection and light is inaccessible.

[39] In Blanqui style: *Instructions pour une prise d'armes*, 1866, https://www.marxists.org/francais/blanqui/1866/instructions.htm, or as Eyal Weizman does, *À travers les murs: l'architecture de la nouvelle guerre urbaine*, (Paris: La Fabrique, 2008).
[40] See <u>The Burial of the Sardine</u>, 1812/1819.)

Heterotopias

The initial goal of this project was to explore the specificities of the border (the DMZ), and to derive from it a working method and forms, which could in turn engender specific readings of it. What brings us the closest to this border, and guides my method of work, is the juxtaposition of discourses that posit the Other as enemy, the irreconcilable interpretations of history, the oppositional-based staging present in this border territory: a heterotopia. The heterotopia has the "power to juxtapose several spaces in a single real place, several locations, which are themselves incompatible."[41] A "heterology" is also played out in this zone, which, in the words of Michel de Certeau, is the discourse of the Other, which is at the same time a discourse about the Other and a discourse through which the Other speaks: *An art of playing on two stages*, a way of evaluating in one place what is missing in the other: Korean history is definitely inscribed within such a setting.

From the border, the site learns about incompatibility and irreconcilability, the current division of the two Koreas, with in counterpoint the nostalgia of reuniting the country and the hope for reconciliation. My site is a heterotopic space with two temporal aims: nostalgia for the past, and the hope of a people whose geopolitical situation threw into the hands of other peoples.

The Invention of the North is deeply rooted in this speculative thought in which form and content, the real and fiction, the order of law and the order of beliefs challenge each other, and question and deconstruct the *fiction expressed in a single voice* that Westerners have composed about the North. The DMZ is a political abstraction and a territorial reality, a border and a non-border, a military construction of space, a staging, an explosive place where truth and untruth are entangled, one of propaganda, conflicts based on

[41] Michel Foucault, *Le corps utopique. Les hétérotopies*, (Fécamp: Nouvelles Editions Lignes, 2009).

appearancesthe place of brother enemies. My site is part of a forward-looking project, one that will develop scenarios that are possible at a given time. Our incapacity to forecast how it will evolve, its infinitely changing nature that undulates according to geopolitical events—out of control today—confers upon it a dynamic, stimulating, and infinitely ephemeral complexion.

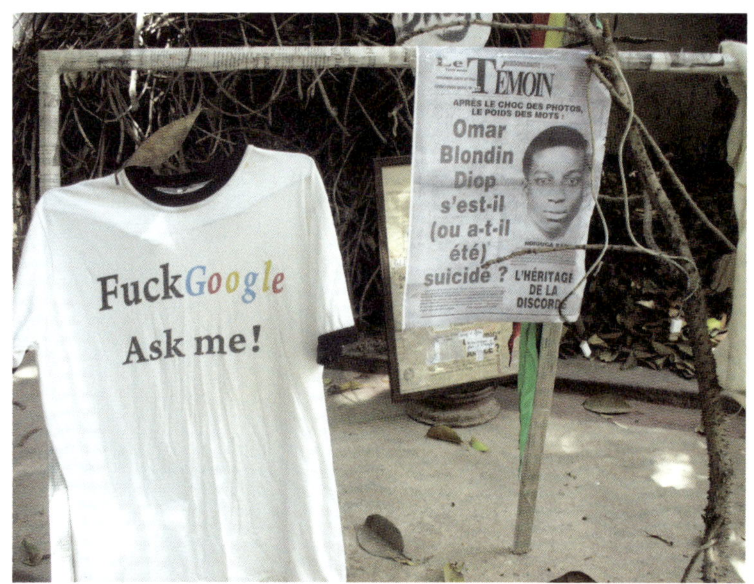

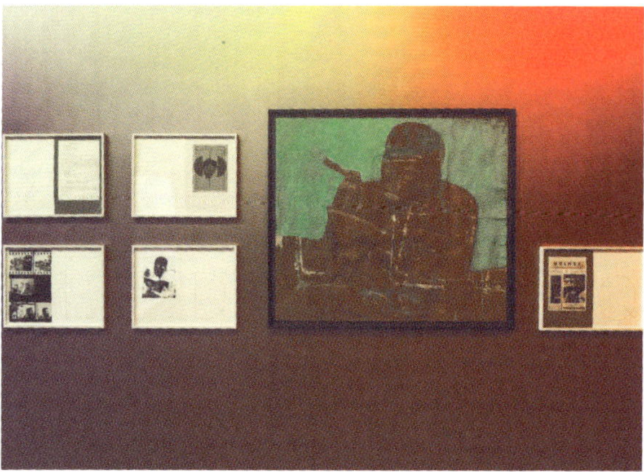

Laboratoire Agit'Art, exhibition *Le Congrès de Minuit*, 2016. Photo: Emmanuelle Chérel.

Vincent Meessen, Index, 26, black and white inkjet print (2015) and Issa Samb, *Omar Blondin Diop*, pastel (c. 1974); View of the exhibition *Sire, je suis de l'ôtre pays*, Wiels, Brussels, 2015, Photo: Sven Laurent.

OUR UNDERSTANDING OF THE WORLD IS BROADER THAN THE WESTERN UNDERSTANDING OF IT.[1]

Thinking with Africa,[2] based on a conception of Africa as its own center, or as Frantz Fanon continually repeated, "its own foundation,"[3] forces us to rewrite art history. Since the end of the 1980s, several factors have led to the revision of historiographic narratives on art. And if we still find ourselves in the midst of the decolonization movement that was needed to reorganize a more egalitarian world and "decolonize our minds," today it is nonetheless commonly admitted that there are entangled modernities,[4] not only a single European modernity extended throughout the entire world. *Thinking with Africa* consists in admitting our lack of knowledge,[5] in breaking with essentialization and deconstructing the concepts linked to the Western invention of this continent, which has been represented as undifferentiated, ahistorical, and determined by tradition and authenticity.[6] It also means taking into consideration the impacts of the new discourses on "African art," which appeared in the 1990s with their complex debates, such as the one on the concept of

---

[1] Boaventura de Sousa Santos, *Renovar la teoria critica y reinventar la emancipacion social (Encuentros en Buenos Aires),* (Buenos Aires: CLACSO 2006), 16.

[2] Achille Mbembe, « L'Afrique Planétaire », De(s)générations, *Penser avec l'Afrique,* n°22, 2015, 19-26.

[3] *Black Skin, White Masks,* trans. Charles Lam Markmann, (New York: Grover Press, 1967), 229.

[4] Shalini Randerian, "Entangled Histories: Civil Society, Caste Solidarities and Legal Pluralism in Post-colonial India," in John Keane (ed.) *Civil society: Berlin perspectives,* (New York: Berghahn Book, 2006).

[5] Catherine Coquery-Vidrovitch, *Petite Histoire de l'Afrique, L'Afrique au Sud du Sahara de la préhistoire à nos jours,* (Paris: La Découverte, 2011), 2016. "*In the 1960s, when French researchers began taking interest in African history, the historians themselves, and not the least of them, indeed, almost all university professors were convinced that Africa did not have a history, because it had not yet been written. (…) This lack of knowledge and this scorn of Blacks go back a long way in history (slave trade, racialism, scientific racism, colonization, and extreme nationalism)." Historical studies increased* in the 1990s, undertaken first by Western scholars, and then by African historians and ones from the African diaspora, including Adame Ba Konaré, John Illife, Joseph Ki-Zerbo, Elikia Mbokolo, and Ibrahima Thioub.

[6] Valentin Y. Mudimbe, *The Invention of Africa: Gnosis, Philosophy, and the Order of Knowledge,* (Bloomington: Indiana University Press, 1988).

modernity,[7] and opposing views,[8] as well as the importance of independent and endogenous African art criticism[9] that advocates for a situated discourse. While these (heterogeneous) historiographies of art have not yet been adequately acknowledged,[10] their implications are nonetheless irreversible. Finally, *Thinking with Africa* enables us to participate in the process that deconstructs representations and knowledges, which is slowly unfolding in Europe, propelled in particular by cultural, postcolonial, and decolonial studies, and to do this while observing the complex historical and present relationships woven between these parts of the world. In other words, to better comprehend the postcolonial present from Europe and to conceive of France as a country in relation to others.

Archipelagic Thinking

My goal in putting together a collection of articles that propose a rereading of art history was to link the artistic scenes in Senegal/Africa and France/Europe, without neglecting to study the postcolonial situation of the field of art in France.[11] These articles present observations, interpretations, and reflections, based on the links they establish between art works and exhibitions, which from the 1970s to the present, are inscribed in anticolonial, political, and social struggles.[12] Writing them enabled us to become familiar with a body of works, authors, questions, positions,

[7] Sandy Prita Meier, « Malaise dans l'authenticité. Écrire les histoires « africaines » et « moyen-orientales » de l'art moderniste », Kantuta Quiros and Aliocha Imhoff (eds.), *Histoires afropolitaines de l'art,* Multitudes, 53, 201, 77-96.

[8] Some lay claims to an essentialized Africanness, while others insist on the plurality of practices. Starting in the late 1980s, the number of studies increased by figures such as M. Adams, P. Ben-Amos, F. N'Goné, S.L. Kasfir, J. Perani, F.T. Smiths, T. Philips, B. Pollack, and John Picton.

[9] Yacouba Konaté, "The Stakes of Art Criticism in Africa," Gallery, no.19, March 1999, 14-15.

[10] Kantuta Quiros and Aliocha Imhoff (eds.), *Histoires afropolitaines de l'art, 53, 36-130.*

[11] Emmanuelle Chérel, Fabienne Dumont (eds.), *L'histoire n'est pas donnée, Art et postcolonialité en France,* (Rennes: PUR, 2016).

[12] *L'énergie radicale de Touki Bouki* (Multitudes), *Relire les modernités africaines pour refonder l'histoire de l'art* (L'Art même), *Que devient l'avant-garde – Personne et les autres,* at the Belgian pavilion, Venice Biennale 2015 (L'Art même), *Les intrigues de la double capture: le contre-jeu au Jeu de la guerre - Notes sur Personne et les autres – Postface to the Scenic Unit* by Vincent Meessen, *All the World's Futures, 56th Venice Biennale* (Errata), *Il faut (re)jouer – L'échiqueté d'Olive Martin et*

situations, and works of art. It also led us to establish the specific hypotheses stated during the projects,[13] notably with the research groups *Ruser l'image*, the Institut Fondamental d'Afrique Noire, the Villa d'Art et Multimédia Kër Thiossane, and the Laboratoire Agit'Art (Issa Samb).[14]

In an international context marked by opposing visions oscillating between global and universalist discourses on art and the necessity to legitimate one's position (a requirement that entails some problematic and excessive forms of behavior), "thinking from the border" signifies to find oneself in an interstitial, ambiguous, and equivocal zone of *otherness*. This approach, which pertains to an attempt to decenter the art historian,[15] functions especially through a spatialization of art history (focusing on the context in which artworks appear), primarily by redefining the tools used to make observations and interpretations, and reconsidering the temporal

Patrick Bernier (…) (Entre-deux), Avec et sans nostalgie (turbulences ou histoire d'un goût très vif pour la liberté 1970-2016), Omar Blondin Diop Reading the Situationist International in 1969 – A photographic archive present in two works: Joe Ouakam - Le Berger d'Ican Ramageli (2015) et Personne et les autres - Postface pour une unité scénique de Vincent Meessen (Venice Biennale, 2015) (forthcoming publication—Mamadou Diouf colloquium, Maureen Murphy (ed.), *Dakar: scènes, acteurs et décors artistiques*, INHA, May 2017), *La cité dans le jour bleu - Paradoxes de la Biennale de Dak'art 12* (forthcoming publication—Revue de l'Observatoire des politiques culturelles), *L'arbre. Lettre à Issa Samb* (Kër Thiossane), *Interview with Vincent Meessen, Une libre association d'individus libres, Centre G. Pompidou* (L'Art même), *Les Plékhanov du Laboratoire Agit'art* (forthcoming publication for a one-day seminar about the Musée Dynamique).

[13] The research took on the form of projects and collaborations. On the one hand, with the *Ruser l'image* group (created in 2012 by the artists Mathieu K. Abonnenc, Patrick Bernier, Latifa Laâbissi, and Olive Martin, and the critics Lotte Arndt and Emmanuelle Chérel), whose work, informed by a postcolonial perspective, seeks to transform the field of art in France; and Malick Ndiaye, an art historian who in 2016 became the acting director of the Théodore Monod African Art Museum, which is linked to the IFAN Museum of African Arts in Dakar, and is also doing research on postcolonial theories. Then, on the other hand, through meetings at the Villa d'Art et Multimédia *Kër Thiossane,* as well as with numerous artists and individuals from the Dakar culture scene, which led to the *Selebe Yoon* workshop and exhibition organized by the *Laboratoire Agit'art* at the Nantes Saint-Nazaire Fine Arts School in March 2016, cinema events, and additional study days in Dakar.

[14] Issa Samb, aka Joe Ouakam, 1945-2017, was an emblematic figure of the Senegalese and African art scene. His multi-faceted Situationist practices, which include assemblage, installation, sculpture, performance, poetry, art criticism, painting, and theater embody a stellar work that combines forms of expression from the African tradition with influences from the international avant-gardes, and the immediacy of political action. He led the Laboratoire Agit'Art from 1974 until his death in April 2017.

[15] In spite of my regular stays in the Senegalese capital since 2007, this project has taken a long time to come into being, due to my doubts concerning the approach to use to describe the artistic practices that emerged in a cultural setting that is not mine. The works of Georges Devereux (*De l'angoisse à la méthode*), Gayatri Spivak, Donna Haraway, Trinh T. Minh-Ha, and others have accompanied me along the way.

question. In other words, my research falls within the scope of a geo-history that attempts to deconstruct the geo-political, geo-epistemological, and geo-esthetic hierarchies inherited from colonial policies, and from the historical narratives associated with Enlightenment philosophers, the grand narratives about progress, modernity and abstract universalism that conceal particularities (as Aimé Césaire has argued[16]). It provides an account of other narratives and visions that question the way of writing art history and consider it to be a palimpsest of discontinuous narratives, contagions, and affinities—in the words of Stuart Hall, entangled and interlocked stories that do not always correspond to each other.[17] In terms of methodology, my research follows what the poet Edouard Glissant calls archipelagic thinking,[18] that is it sketches out, from different angles, cultural and intellectual circuits, areas of contact, sharing, and meeting, but also ones where there are frictions, differences, and creolizations. It pays attention to wars of position and the forms of solidarity established internationally between esthetic, social, and political struggles. The form of my essay has no ambition to analyze exhaustively the subject it tackles: free associations transgress certain norms, while defining a singular and subjective territory, in an attempt to describe the realities and paradoxes of the field of international contemporary art.

On the Political and Social Roles of Art from Independence until Today

The 2014 rescreening in movie theaters of Djibril Diop Mambety's *Touki Bouki* (1973), just after Mati Diop's short film *Mille soleils* was

[16.]Aimé Césaire, "Letter of Resignation from the Communist Party," 1956,
 https://readingfanon.blogspot.com/2011/06/aime-cesaires-letter-of-resignatio.
[17.]Stuart Hall, "When was 'the Post-colonial'?:Thinking at the Limit," in Iain Chambers and Lidia Curti (eds.), *The Post-Colonial Question: Common Skies, Divided Horizons*, (London: Routledge, 1996), 242-260.
[18] "Archipelagic thinking is well suited to the ways of our worlds. It draws on their ambiguous, fragile and drifting nature. It is in accord with the practice of diversion which is not the same as flight or rejection. It acknowledges the contributions made by the imagination of the Trace, which it approves. Does that mean to refuse to govern oneself? No, it means to be in harmony with what in this world is spread out in archipelagos, these sorts of diversity in space, which nonetheless connect shores and blend different horizons. We realize what was continental, dense and weighing us down, in the sumptuous thought (…)

released (2013), showcased a very singular example of the invention of a certain kind of cinema in Africa. With its critical imagination and radical poetics, this outstanding movie reappropriates multiple sources, particularly international ones, and displays undeniable formal freedom. Mambety's subtle observations of the lives of his contemporaries—a rapidly changing Senegalese society, made up of antagonistic realities stemming from colonization and its aftermath (contradictory aspirations, hybrid references, internal conflicts) and of new cultural identities—as well as his insightful social critique and his condemnation of the relationships France has had with its former African colonies—seem to be good sources for meetings, research, and discussions.

Malick Ndiaye[19] was given carte blanche by *Ruser l'image* for the first day of reflections, "Afterimage—Methodological Reflections on the New Visualities," held at the Théodore Monod Museum, and which aimed to make the participants more knowledgeable about the artistic and cinematographic scene in Senegal. They were able to meet with and listen to this active scene, which is undergoing transformations and also confronted with many problems including a lack of art theory and art history courses at the university, inadequate critical debate, gaps in the recent theoretical tools, fragile national cultural policies, and the difficulties encountered by artists who would like to show their works. Likewise, the artists who were present insisted on the weakening of cinema,[20] and of its political impact, which were being supplanted by

(…) systems that have until now governed the History of the humanities, and which are no longer adequate for expressing our shards or our histories, nor our no less sumptuous wanderings" *Le traité du tout monde*. (Paris: Gallimard, 2013).

[19] He invited participants to leave behind their visions centered around the rereading of the historical relations between our two countries. Notwithstanding the obvious need to reassess colonial history in France, this colonial history has tended to fade into the background in Senegal over the past decade (even if the link between France and Senegal remains the subject of great discussion in Senegal, as witnessed during the debate concerning the West African CFA franc).

[20] The Awa is the only movie theater built during the period of Senegalese independence that remains open. There are only three places to watch movies in Dakar. The Senegalese government recently set up a substantial fund to promote the cinema and audiovisual industry.

video clips on the net and the diktats of the Western cinema industry. They also expressed their critiques of the State, of economic logics, and of the dominant imported representations, as well as their concerns about their status and social role. The question of artists' responsibility vis-à-vis their communities was also commented upon at length by the artist Fatou Kande Senghor and the filmmaker Moussa Sene Absa, who evoked through very different points of view, their preoccupations concerning the current issues in Senegalese society, including its rapidly occurring economic, social and cultural transformations driven by the impacts of globalization, the place of religion, immigration, the situation of women and of women artists, the control of sexuality, the need to redefine a project for society, and democratic vigilance. They insisted on the importance of a constant link with the young generations, on the virtues of popular education and artistic forms that could dialogue with social realities and the population. They argued that it was necessary to let Africa tell its own stories and make its own images, just as their movies constitute a constant critique of their society.[21] Members of the association *Ruser l'image* considered the day to be quite uncomfortable. It put us face to face with our situation as foreigners (or even as representatives of the "winning side"), to discursive methods, realities, points of view, analyses, debates, and practices (at times rather eclectic), which we did not know, and whose stakes were difficult to ascertain. It also led us to confirm our interest in artistic propositions that make us reflect on the political and social roles of art. As for Malick Ndiaye, he decided to initiate a program of monthly seminars focusing on cultural policies, based on the strategy of bringing together people involved in the artistic and cultural scene in Senegal. These seminars (which have since become an indispensable institution) seek to break down the barriers between artists, academics, and cultural administrators, and to generate new dynamics through a transversal approach, to open up new projects, and to participate in a process that can redefine

[21] The artist painter Kiné Awa, and the art historian Babacar Mbaye Diop also attended the event.

public missions as well as in a movement that can rewrite historiographic and museographic narratives.

Subsequent work focused on initiatives proposed by artistic and cultural actors who define the place of culture and art as the space of social and political transformations. Conversations with artists such as Issa Samb, Viyé Diba, Fatou Kandé Senghor, and Kan Si enabled us to improve our knowledge of art history since the independence of former colonies and to identify avenues of inquiry. It was also very interesting to meet other key actors (from rap, hip hop, and theater), who have also created continuously renewed and effective collective forms of art over the past 30 years. They have instituted processes for democratic watch (embodied by the *Y'en a marre* movement in 2011[22]), self-representation (particularly in the outer cities), dialogue, support, and expression for the youth. Our discussions with some of them (*Africulture urbaine*, *Plan B*, *Kaddu Yaraax*, *Espoir de la Banlieue*, and *Journal rappé*) led us to attempt to recontextualize their approaches by seeking their models and historical sources. An anthropological study carried out in May 2015 for *Kër Thiossane*[23] gave us the opportunity to better understand certain social realities concerning membership/citizenship/conventions in public spaces[24]) as well as the artistic scene in Dakar. *Kër Thiossane* is one of the new private cultural projects, like *Raw Material,* and *Les petites pierres*, which as of the 2000s, sought to make up for the lack of places where people could show their art and engage in reflection. They aimed to question the institutions set up by the postcolonial state and their

[22] *Y'en a marre* (Fed up), a protest movement that originated in rap, mobilized the youth in 2011 against a third term of office for then incumbent President Abdoulaye Wade, which would have been contrary to the constitution.

[23] A study on the reception of the project to make a collective garden and learning commons in the *Sicap liberté – jet d'eau* district.

[24] Mamadou Diouf, Rosalind Fredericks, *Les arts de la citoyenneté au Sénégal, Espaces contestés et civilités urbaines*, (Paris: Karthala, 2013). See also the round table discussion (*Agir le Bien Commun/ Villes africaines, espaces d'émancipation et réinvention de soi*) organized in Kër Thiossane during the 2016 Dak'art biennial, with Mamadou Diouf, Felwine Sarr, Cheikh Ndiaye, Armin Kane, Piniang, and Emmanuelle Chérel.

92

centralizing model. Whereas since the 1960s, the perception and comprehension of artistic practices were sometimes still restricted to the philosophical lyricism of Léopold S. Senghor,[25] these initiatives aimed to break with this understanding of art limited to esthetics and emotion, which isolates it from social and political concepts and debates, and produced several generations of spectators who perceived art as entertainment and as an embellishing activity. Preoccupied by the contribution of art to the emancipation of citizens in a difficult social context, and by the emergence of critical thinking within civil society, they attempted to revive the debate on the role of art in a contemporary African society that was experiencing irreversible social transformations.

Rereading the History of the Avant-gardes

Little by little, the observation of a collective ignorance of art history and of the political and cultural realities since the Independence was confirmed. As Malick Ndiaye has insisted, these histories remain to be written:[26] a phenomenon linked, among other things, to the absence of archives.[27] For example, Jean-Charles Tall, Director of the Dakar University Architecture School, reminded us about the *Front culturel sénégalais* (1975-1987), a clandestine movement opposed to Senghor's politics, and whose history has remained in the shadows up to the present day,[28] but which influenced many artists and stirred up society. This discussion brought us back to the *Kër Thiossane* meeting of the former members of the *Front culturel sénégalais*[29] in order to reconsider its history, operating methods, and productions (widely

[25] A rereading of Senghor's project is in progress. See for example the discussions during the colloquium *Dakar: scènes, acteurs et décors artistiques,* INHA, Columbia University, Université Paris 1, 2017.
[26] There are no Art History Departments in Senegalese universities, and few individuals have formal education in this field of study.
[27] Day-long seminar *What Museums for Senegal in the 21st Century?* April 12, 2107, IFAN, organized by Malick Ndiaye and Emmanuelle Chérel.
[28] Fadel Barro, one of the leaders of *Y'en a marre*, expressed his amazement about the fact that this history, which he did not know, had not been transmitted.
[29] *Agir le Bien Commun* no. 2, https://www.youtube.com/watch?v=U_XLj3ithZ4.

disseminated songs and poetry), which were performed on this occasion by young slammers (*Vendredi Slam*).

These preoccupations were not unrelated to the research being carried out by Vincent Meessen on the rereading of the history of the artistic avant-gardes in the framework of his exhibition *Personne et les autres* for the Belgian Pavilion at the 2015 Venice Biennale. This pavilion presented Omar Blondin Diop, a young Senegalese anti-colonial militant who was a member of the Situationist International and played in Godard's movie *La chinoise* (1967). On display was also Olive Martin and Patrick Bernier's *L'échiqueté,*[30] a version of chess that confronts us with our cultural, political and psychic ambiguities stemming from colonization. A more pragmatic example is the approach adopted by the *Rendez-vous demain* initiative,[31] stemming from the desire to reflect collectively upon the social and political situation expressed through the attacks against the satirical newspaper *Charlie Hebdo*. It questions both representations and their history, the conditions in which images appear, are received, and circulate in our current globalized context, the systems invented by artists to question and act upon a pluralistic democracy, as well as the role of popular education.[32]

From Dakar to Nantes, our exchanges with the artists Issa Samb and Ican Ramageli[33] enabled us to better comprehend the history of the Laboratoire Agit'art and how it was engaged in 2016. Founded in 1973, this avant-garde and multidisciplinary laboratory (theater, performance, painting, and more), which brought together major artists such as El Hadji Sy, Amadou Sow, Djibril Diop Mambety, and

---

[30] Presented at *Personne et les autres*.

[31] Born in Nantes, this collective initiative brings together many people for a wide range of events.

[32] See also E. Chérel (ed.), Revue 303, no. 137, *Le dessin de presse*.

[33] Ican Ramageli is a young artist who like many Senegalese artists has a wide range of artistic practices ranging from painting to video, photography, performance, and music. A member of the Laboratoire Agit'Art, he made the video *Joe Ouakam - Le Berger* (35 min., 2013). In 2014, he participated in the exhibition-performance *Sans Rien* with Issa Samb, as well as an eponymous film (45 min., 2015), and then *Regards sur la ville,* in the framework of the event *Partcours 2015, Le Congrès de Minuit* (Biennale 2016) and *Zone d'Autonomie Artistique, Partcours 2016*.

Bouna Medoune Seye rejected the essentialist and formalist view of art propounded by the *École de Dakar*, which was informed by Léopold Sedar Senghor's philosophy of negritude, in favor of a collective and collaborative approach to art. By focusing on the contingent nature of actions, engaging in practices with installations, performances, and public interventions based on experimentation, agitation, and the process, the Laboratoire Agit'art was critiquing institutional power, defending esthetic and democratic pluralism, and pursuing its interest in social and political questions. It generated a symbiosis between artistic and social domains in Senegal, by establishing a new combination of foreign and local ideas and forms, that is, a new synthesis of African[34] and Western[35] points of references. Its subversive, critical, and experimental positions and practices have had major impacts on the artistic scene and democratic life over the past forty years.[36]

Simultaneously, the text *Avec et sans nostalgie (turbulences ou histoire d'un goût très vif pour la liberté 1970-2016 (With and Without Nostalgia (Turmoil or the Story of a Very Pronounced Taste for Freedom 1970-2016))* was written in the form of notes, which established avenues of inquiry and relations that were created from Independence (1960) to the present day between the sphere of art, left-wing political minorities in Senegal, and the situation in France, characterized by the defeat of Third-Worldism, and the survival of an a-temporal vision of Africa. This text was read in December 2016 during the *Wiwildu* exhibition featuring works by Patrick Bernier and Olive Martin at the

[34] See Abdou Sylla, *Création et imitation dans l'Art africain,* (Dakar: Cheikh Anta Diop University, 1988).
[35] On the practices of the Laboratoire Agit'Art, its dialogues within the Senegalese context with Western avant-garde movements such as Surrealism and Situationism, and the writing of Georgi Plekhanov and Antonin Artaud, as well as its position between tradition, borrowing, and inventions, see Elisabeth Harney, "Laboratories of Avant-gardism," in *Senghor's Shadow art, politics and the Avant-garde in Sénégal,* 1960-1995, (Durham, London: Duke University Press, 2004), 105-140.
[36] With the students from the Nantes School of Art, we were confronted with the radical positions of Issa Samb and Ican Ramageli, who in response to the current issues in society were still seeking to stir up the art scene, defend other visions and forms of knowledge, and pursue dialogues with others, social struggles, the transmission of energies and ideas, the relations linking all people and to others, as well as a form of disobedience by striving to "create art" in all aspects of life.

Grand Café contemporary art center in Saint-Nazaire.[37] It complemented the mural assemblage of archives that created links between the history of the *Ancerville* (a cruise ship filmed in *Touki Bouki),* the city of Saint-Nazaire (where the boat was built), and Africa-China relations (the *Ancerville* is now a restaurant in China). Its narrative configuration, constructed with the filmmaker Mamadou Khouma Gueye, sketches out a complex territory that renders visible coincidences and convolutions between historical facts and artworks such as films, songs, and text, which were critical of Senghor's politics. These artists aimed to achieve social transformation through artistic, cultural, and poetic activism, to raise awareness and consciousness in line with the ideologies and thoughts shared by young people internationally (May 1968, Sekou Touré, Marxism-Leninism, the Situationists, the Tricontinental Conference, the Black Panthers, and Maoism and the cultural revolution). Such practices, which include popular education through art, and the engagement of artists, have been redeployed and reinvented over the past forty years. This text—an incomplete and subjective narrative—resonated unexpectedly with a letter written by Issa Samb in 2012 to Malal Talla, (Fou malade),[38] a member of *Y'en a marre* and to the youth of 1988. Issa Samb links the *Y'en a marre* movement to Omar Blondin Diop, a symbol of the struggle of the 1970s, and underlines the importance of the engagement of this youth, for the people, and how they fit into a genealogy of struggle. However, he warns of the dangers for artists to leave behind their art for "*street politics*" and political parties. He invites them to avoid the drama of the instrumentalization of revolution by alluding to the photograph of a demonstrator standing near a trace of human blood: "what is to be seen resembles the blood in Djibril Diop's *Touki Bouki.*" His letter concludes with the affirmation that the revolution will be brought about by people because the *"game played*

[37] In the framework of an invitation made by the group *Ruser l'image.*
[38] Published in the very beautiful catalogue that recounts the events of 2012, *Chronique d'une révolte, photographies d'une saison de protestation,* Raw Material, (Berlin: Haus der Kulturen des Welt, 2012).

at the National Assembly does not lead to any change. It is not a game of chess, because in chess when a piece moves off a square all of the others see their reciprocal position change, like in Yoot)."[39]

Apprehending a Singular Place of Enunciation

At the Institut Fondamental d'Afrique Noire, the one-day seminar *Enseignement de l'art, prospective et invention pédagogique. Comment? Pour qui? Quelles finalités? (Teaching Art, Prospects and Pedagogical Innovation. How? For Whom? For What Purposes?)* was a new attempt to bring together people involved in the Senegalese art scene through an exploration of the social role of art based on a wide range of original teaching practices. The goal was to showcase at the university different practices that were very common in Senegal from the visual arts, theater, cinema, slam, rap journals, and graffiti,[40] and opposing views (on the place of the individual, religion, and nature[41]). Another goal was to bring together people from institutions (Fine Arts School), associations (Plan B), and private initiatives (an Architectural school, and the *Portes et passages* project), from different generations, and from different urban and social environments (downtown/outer city). The final goal was to showcase practices that make up for what the public establishments

[39] Issa Samb goes on to say: *"You have nothing to do with that political system, the system of the leaders of the opposition, or of civil society organizations, or of human rightsism and the retrograde ideologies simmered in Senegalese (or okra) sauce, or of NGOs, bankrolled by Western democracies and Eastern dictatorships. This generation which is revolting is the one that is continuing 1968, the generation of Omar Blondin Diop and company, the generation of those who one day realized that too much is too much, that the liberal political and economic system is fundamentally unfair because in that world in which the youth must resort to their own resourcefulness to make a place for themselves, some transforming themselves into street vendors, others into migrants, those who gamble in Sandaga to crush their brothers for a bit of money or become talibé, who burn up what is left of their youth already damaged by drugs, and here is the suffering of those who shout out their youth, their rage of having no perspectives in the outer cities other than the anguish of their shanties and a rhythm of life with three daily teas. (…) the little dot with a hood far away, over there, can you see it? It's me! It's you, no it's me, and all the others."*

[40] The visual artists Issa Samb, Ican Ramageli, Viyé Diba, Fatou Kandé Senghor, Kan Si, and Mushana Ali, the graffiti artist Docta, the filmmakers from Plan B, Vendredi Slam, Journal Rappé, and the theater forum, Kaadu Yaarax. *le peuple qui manque* and I were the only foreign contributors (May 2016).

[41] See for example the exchange between Mushana Ali and Koyo Kouoh.

cannot offer (because their programs are so distant from the cultural and social realities in Senegal, their lack of means and limited enrolment capacity, which excludes people who do not live in the downtown area). This seminar aimed to dismantle hierarchies, and was imagined to be a working space conceived of as a place of agonisms and for engaging in complex negotiations based on tolerance and an openness to debate which would enable the emergence of new practices and ideas. Numerous contributions emphasized the notion of cultural memory,[42] that is a collective memory composed of a specific inventory of texts, images, and rites through which a particular society expresses its own conception of itself : a memory that does not only shape ideas concerning the past, but a society's identity. These interventions insisted in particular on the need to establish other bodies of knowledge that include traditional knowledge and know-how, which often correspond better to the realities of the country, and to redefine the criteria used to judge works, in particular, by studying how they are related to social and cultural practices such as exchanges, rites, beliefs, imagination, and conceptions of the body, action, and orality). The speakers expressed their desire to have the needs better identified (particularly those of the youth from the outer city, because it is crucial to better understand their models and systems of representation, including their relationship to religion as well as to internet/Facebook, and their identification strategies). They also insisted that we must question the term "development" and the logic that shapes our economic policies and the phenomena linked to globalization. For example, the artist Viyé Diba underlined the consequences of International Monetary Fund structural adjustment plans in the 1980s on the Senegalese society and art world. Many speakers insisted on the importance of transforming representations and giving consideration to the initiatives taken in the outer cities. At the same time as they reaffirmed that art and how we teach it must raise awareness about the social context and the

---

[42] Jan and Aleida Assmann, *Der lange Schatten der Vergangenheit,* (Munich: C.H. Beck, 2006).

difficulties in it, the various interventions all defined art as the work of an individual in a given situation in a society, and artistic production as something linked to the social project and system of production (*What can we do when we are not in charge of them? How can tactical visual wealth be created?*).

This day-long seminar brought to light the gaps between the artistic works displayed at the Dak'Art biennial in 2016 and what was at that time important in the Senegalese art scene.[43] Globalization in the art world sometimes leads people to believe that thought, theories, and artworks circulate rapidly, a belief inspired by the desire to move beyond all forms of essentialism and culturalism, and to further develop the transnational phenomena that generated the counter-culture of modernity (such as Pan-Africanism). This vision, however, by defending the idea that an international art field exists—as never before—at a crossroads of hybridity, runs the risk of making us miss out on more complex phenomena. As Nestor Garcia Canclini has written, the main problem in terms of global interactions today is the tension between cultural homogenization and cultural heterogenization:

> *I see in irreverent hybrids opportunities to relativize the religious, political, national, ethnic, and artistic fundamentalisms that establish absolute values for certain forms of heritage while discriminating against others. But I also wonder if extreme discontinuity as a perceptual habit, as well as the decreasing number of occasions for understanding how the significations still surviving in certain traditions are re-elaborated, so as to influence their change, does not increase the power usurped by those who are constantly concerned about comprehending and controlling the major networks of objects and significations: multinationals and governments.*[44]

[43] The contributions underlined the lack of any real relationship between the biennial, the city, and its art scene, as well as the absence of any government policy to truly support the artists between the biennials. For instance, there is no contemporary art museum in Dakar.

[44] Nestor Garcia Canclini, "Cultures Hybrides, stratégies pour entrer et sortir de la modernité", cited in Sophie Orlando and Catherine Grenier (eds.), *Art et mondialisation, Décentrements, anthologie de textes de 1950 à nos jours,* (Paris: Centre G. Pompidou, 2013), 99.

In other words, while the new global economy must be seen as a complex capitalist order, which is both disjunctive and, in some ways, overlapping,[45] cosmopolitan desires or those for a new cultural policy based on difference (Cornel West) must be analyzed in terms of the complex relations between global culture and local cultures (Mike Fearthestone). Thus, for example, the extremely mobile discourses espoused for the length of an art Biennale, by reviews or nomadic curatorial discursive platforms can reenact relationships meant to conceal realities. While in such a context, we must avoid the pitfalls of "topographic nativism," binary vision *"external discourse/internal discourse"* (Paulin Hountondji), and strategic essentialism (Gayatri S. Spivak), we cannot however deny that there is a "localization" and a "positionality" of works and texts, which emerge from a singular place of enunciation, and firmly reiterate the need to be understood as such. Such a denial would mean to forget the geo-epistemic power relations that give birth to them, and would continue to obliterate their existences as politically situated and constituted discourses.

Temporal Questions

This rereading of history was continued through the analysis of the presence of the same image, a photographic archive— *Omar Blondin Diop Reading the Situationist International in 1969*—in two works: the film *Joe Ouakam - Le Berger* (2015) by Ican Ramageli (starring Issa Samb), and *Personne et les autres - Postface to the Scenic Unit* by Vincent Meessen (2015). While the question of archives has been given considerable attention in the field of art over the past ten years, and archival art[46] shares the same strong interest as the reflections on the postcolonial condition for what is fragmentary and transgressive, the issue becomes more complex when we consider that there are orders of time that vary according to the times and places. To understand the

[45] According to Scott Lash and John Urry, the new global world economy cannot be understood in terms of center-periphery models, but is generated by disorganized capitalism. *The End of Organized Capitalism*, (Madison: University of Wisconsin Press, 1987).
[46] Hal Foster, "An Archival Impulse," October, Vol. 110, (Fall 2004): 3-24.

utilization of archives in contemporary art in Africa, it is necessary to consider the question of time in terms of its diversity by taking account of the "historicity regimes"[47] of African societies. In other words, the resurgence of the emblematic figure Omar Blondin Diop, and the rereading of the influence of non-Western intellectuals in avant-garde movements, such as the Situationist International, are expressed through different relationships to the "historical" document, to time, and to History.

In Dakar, in the Jules Ferry courtyard, filmed by Ican Ramageli, the photograph of Omar Blondin Diop where Issa Samb lived and had his studio much as the other totems erected in memory of certain people, did not symbolize the past, but the present. This vision results from the cultural and personal relationship Issa Samb had with death:

> This is what my work on death means: the people I've known and with whom I've shared my journey, are not gone. They're here with me. Every day. (…) For the Lébous, the deceased are not dead. They're here. They're not memories. Some people are indeed bothered by this aspect of my work. (…) Death is a presence. It does not evoke the past. Death is born at the heart of life. Because it is from death—the inanimate— that the animate is born. It's not a cult, but it's very powerful from an ontological point of view. Only those who don't want to hear about it, think it's a belief. I firmly believe that Djibril (Mambety Diop) and all the others you see here, their bodies are gone, but their spirits remain. (…) And this is not to be ascribed to religious beliefs either. No! No! It's ourselves and the emotions we have, the feelings nourished with regard to people when we speak about them. It's our path. It's what we will be doing tomorrow.[48]

[47] A society's "historicity regimes" translate its temporal order, and the ways it relates to the past, present, and future. François Hartog, *Régimes d'historicité: Présentisme et expériences du temps,* (Paris: Seuil, 2003).

[48] Issa Samb, *Word! Word? Word! Issa Samb and the Undecipherable Form*, (Berlin, Dakar, Oslo: Sternberg Press, OCA, 2013), 18 (my adaptation).

In the small black volume *Personne et les autres - Postface to the Scenic Unit* designed by Vincent Meessen, this image also re-engages with history by re-establishing links between the North and the South. It conjures up specters,[49] and participates in a new dialogue linking facts, artworks, and historical protagonists. Yet this conversation with the dead, while it stems from taking into consideration pluralistic modes of existence,[50] is also linked to Anselm Franke's revision of animism,[51] which expresses another ontological vision.

This research thus obliges us to reconsider the fact that there is a permanent injunction at the international scale to be contemporary,[52] which supports the illusion of a world in which everyone is living in the same historical time and in which and the different times are supposedly in concordance with each other. This injunction conceals temporal differences and a war between different times. The African continent is subjected to contradictory representations. In order to escape from two illusions, an ethnographic allochrony[53] and contemporary euphoria (both equally violent, because they support the notion that the future powered by global neoliberal capitalism will be African), Felwine Sarr[54] observes that the writing of history in Africa, and especially that of the future, requires African societies to produce their own metaphors of the future. They must refuse to be dominated by the modern Western episteme and assert another perspective of social life grounded in other mythological worlds. For Sarr, as for Valentin Y. Mudimbe, Kwasi Wiredu, and Ngugi Wa Thiong'o, this would involve moving beyond mimesis, defining African modernities, succeeding in telling their own stories and especially in thinking of themselves beyond the civilizational injunctions of others, and rediscovering the potentialties of time, in order to open up the possibility of a

[49] T. J. Demos *Return to the Postcolony: Specters of Colonialism in Contemporary Art*, (Berlin: Sternberg Press, 2013).
[50] Bruno Latour, Enquête sur les modes d'existence. Une anthropologie des modernes, (Paris: La Découverte, 2012).
[51] Anselm Franke, *Animism: Notes on an Exhibition*, www.e-flux.com/.../animism-notes-on-an-exhibition.
[52] François Hartog, *Régimes d'historicité.*
[53] Johannes Fabian, *Le Temps et les autres: Comment l'anthropologie construit son objet,* (Paris: Anacharsis, 2006).
[54] Felwine Sarr, *Afrotopia,* (Paris: Rey, 2016).

future by drawing on endogenous forms of knowledge in particular[55] and on the particular gnoseological criteria of these cultures (Wole Soyinka):

> *Afrocontemporeneity is the present moment, the psychological continuum of what Africans experience. It incorporates their past, and portends their future, which must be thought of in a way that grasps all of its significations. The development of new social and political theories that reflect the current trends in African societies is necessary.*[56]

This vision requires us to unlearn our understanding of history as a process of development moving toward a singular future. It leads us to conceive "a potential regime,"[57] that is knots of time that interweave the past, the present, and the future. It invites us to accept a dialectical contemporary conception,[58] which would seek to construct multiple temporalities with a political purpose, and to consider that *"the map of critical terminology, the map of art and of politics will have to be redrawn on the basis of a new semantics of timescules, archipelagic space-times, interpolating and overlapping times."*[59] The archival pulsion might open up a realm of possibilities thereby creating a dynamic and forward-looking historicity. In this perspective, if *"according to the emancipatory scripts and past utopias, the future were what will be, the future about which we are now speaking is everything that can happen, everything that could be, everything that may come to be."*[60]

Third Space

This vast re-writing project is just beginning in Africa, the West, and the rest of the world. To avoid the pitfalls of a vision that only

---

[55] Paulin Hountoundji (ed.), *Les savoirs endogènes: Pistes pour une recherche*, (Dakar: Codesria, 1994).

[56] Sarr, *Afrotopia*, 40.

[57] Aliocha Imhoff and Kantuta Quiros, « Casting Temporel », in Camille de Toledo, Aliocha Imhoff, and Kantuta Quiros, *Les potentiels du temps, art et politique,* (Paris: Manuelle Editions, 2016), 85.

[58] Claire Bishop, *Radical Museology or, What's Contemporary in Museums of Contemporary Art?,* (London: Koenig Books, 2013).

[59] Imhoff and Quiros, *Les potentiels,* 97.

[60] Imhoff and Quiros, *Les potentiels.* Thinking the possible as an operation that seizes the potentiality of the current situation in order to stimulate agency.

promotes major international events,[61] and work against the very mechanisms that produced a monopolistic definition of universal standards and attempted to conceal social, religious, cultural and gender differences in the name of esthetic autonomy and a universal language of forms, but also to move beyond visions focused on policies of difference and diversity, research must continue to contextualize artistic and cultural practices in more precise locations. Completely eliminating the historical frame and the specific place from which an artist speaks impoverishes the esthetic experience and especially negates the right of art to participate in the construction of reality. However, this perspective also obliges us to comprehend how artistic practices can be considered as discursive strategies in a constantly changing international network, within old and new forms of territoriality. That process leads to showing their various genealogies and underscores the complex contradictions and tensions activated by modernity and its different sites of enunciation.

The research approach I have adopted is marked by a form of engagement that results from the need to understand and act, based on a continual movement between two positions—internal and external—, within what Homi K. Bhabha calls a *third space*, in which experience and hermeneutics work in synergy. According to Bhabha, *"Although it is unrepresentable, the third space constitutes the discursive conditions of enunciation that attest to the fact that meaning and cultural symbols do not have any primordial unity or fixity, and that the same signs can be appropriated, translated, rehistoricized and reinterpreted."*[62] It is the space of hybridity, a space open to the influence of opposites and translation, in which none of the binary divisions or antagonisms typical of modern conceptions function. Yet it is also the space of subversion and transgression. It authorizes what Bhabha calls *"negotiation,"* and negotiation and translation are the means for making something new emerge.

---

[61] What can we say about the fashion of contemporary African art that is unfurling in France with *100% Afrique* at La Villette, whose title continues to cultivate the myths of authenticity and a poster that represents Africa with an odalisque?

[62] Homi K. Bhabha, *Les lieux de la culture, pour une théorie postcoloniale*, (Paris: Payot, 2007), 65.

More specifically Bhabha describes the theoretical statement as something that emerges within the play on an ambivalence that is an integral component of its own linguistic and cultural system. In other words, the theoretical statement operates in a two-way dialogical movement within which it is part of a dialectics (negotiation) of antagonistic and contradictory arguments. It opens up *"hybrid sites and combat objectives, which destroy those negative polarities between knowledge and its objects, theory and practical-political reason."*[63] In this sense, the researcher's situation seems to be close here to that of a player of *L'échiqueté (Checkered Chess),* the game invented by Olive Martin and Patrick Bernier:

> The uncomfortable moment links the traumatic ambivalences of a personal psychic history to the wider disjunctions of political existence. (...) Living in the uncomfortable world, finding its ambivalences and ambiguities employed in the house of fiction, or its separation and rupture represented in the work of art, is also the assertion of a profound desire for social solidarity.[64]

P.S.: "We no longer have a universal system that establishes the order upon which the world must be aligned, we are in the age of a lateral universal, which has from our origins developed in the plurality of languages. We are at a time in which we must learn to identify the universal through translation. (…) The universal is a horizon that is proposed from a position of postcoloniality. It is only today, embedded in postcoloniality, that we have the capacity to seriously think a universal that will not be imposed from above."[65]

---

[63] Bhabha, 64.
[64] Bhabha, 43 and 54.
[65] Souleymane Bachir Diagne, « Du mouvement vers l'universel », *De(s)générations, Penser avec l'Afrique,* n° 22, 2015, 19-26.

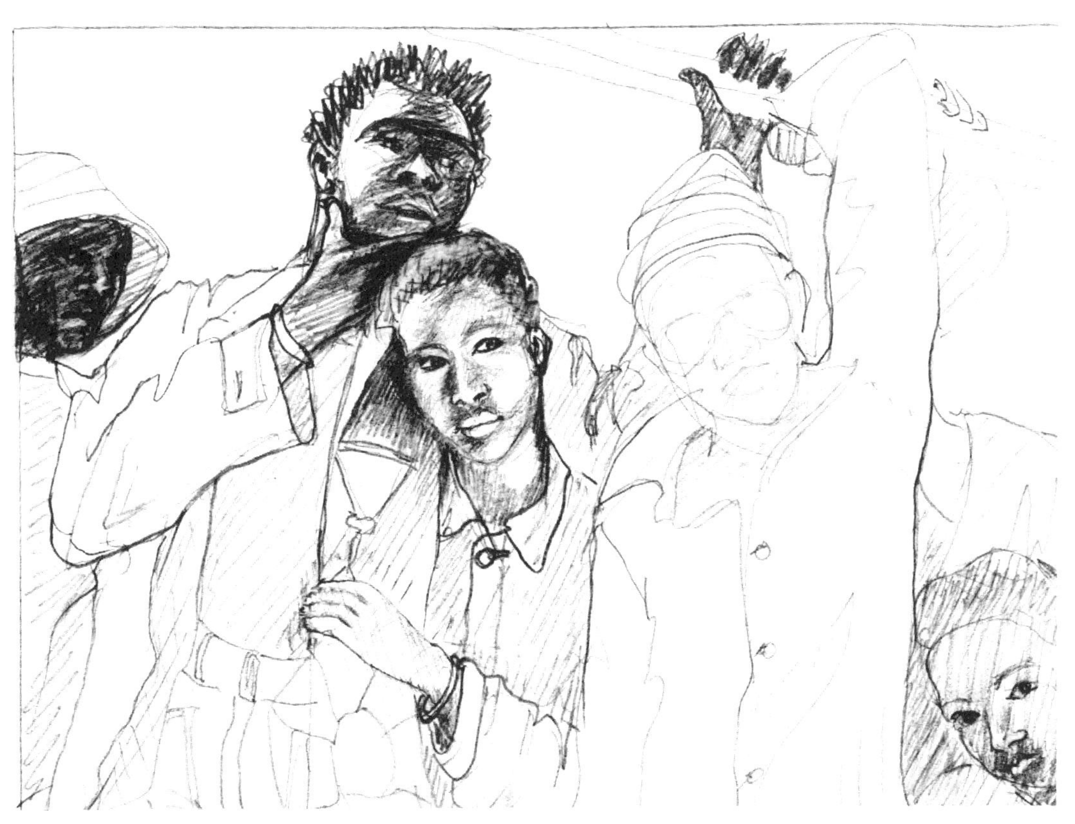

Olive Martin, *Touki Bouki*, drawing, Multitudes no. 56, 2015 @courtesy of the artist.

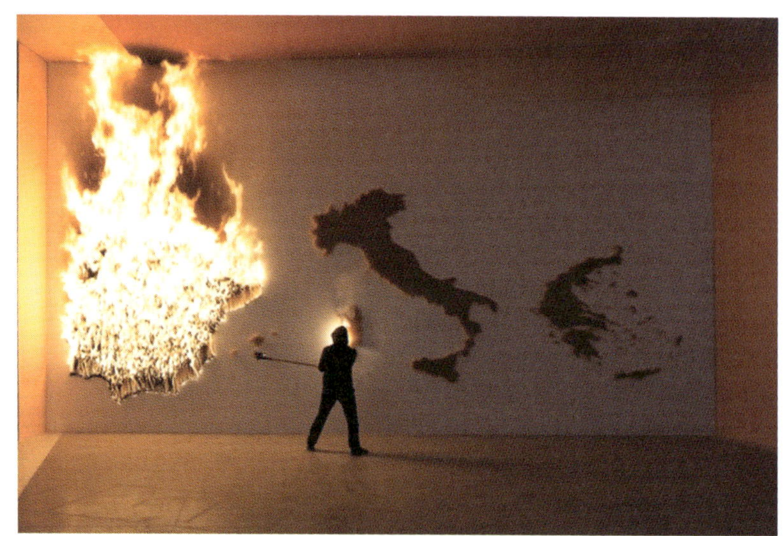

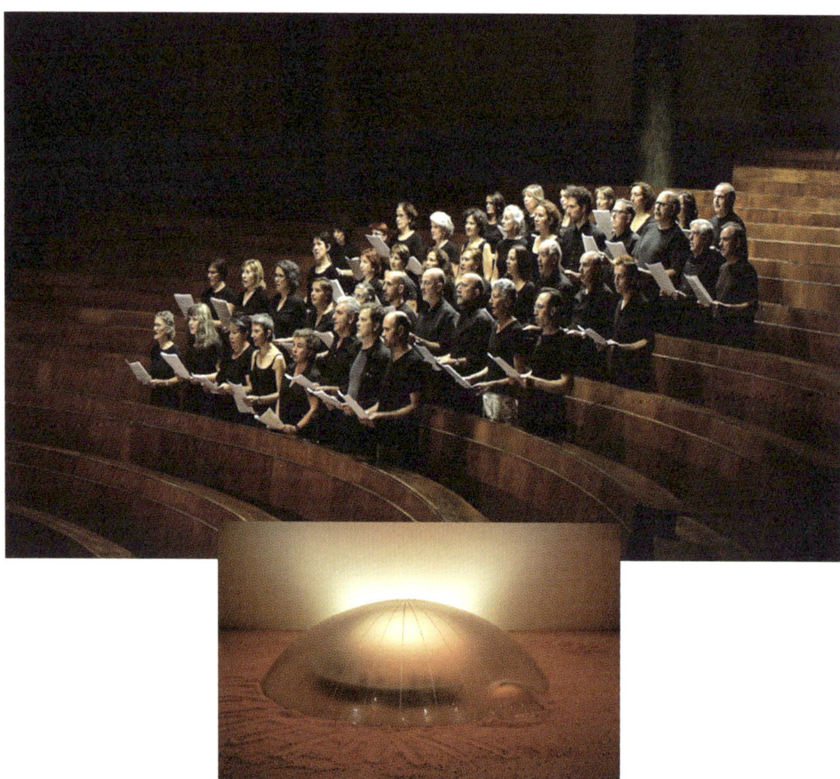

Claire Fontaine, *P.I.G.S.*, installation, 2012 @courtesy of the artist.
Marco Godoy, *Reclamar el eco,* performance, 2012 @ courtesy of the artist.
Peter Sloterdijk, Gesa Mueller von der Haegen, and Dierk Jordan, *Pneumatic Parliament*, sculpture, 2005.

BARCELONA EN COMÙ: QUESTIONS FACING A NEW BRAND OF POLITICAL ACTION

Our sociological inquiry emerged in the process of crossing the border between France and Catalonia in 2016. Our objective was to understand the political, social, and activist trajectories of certain individuals who were elected to the new Barcelona municipal government (and of their supporters) as closely as possible to their personal dimensions. Having won the elections, in May 2015, in what the European media considered to be quite a surprising victory, Ada Colau, a figure from the social movements that were fighting against housing evictions, became the mayor of Barcelona and was steadfastly determined to "deglobalize" the city.

We decided to go meet this new political generation, which had been shaped by the "not in our name" intellectual and activist contexts of the early 2000s, and won over to the methods of empowerment and continuous deliberation, often learned in the framework of their professional experience in cooperation and development networks in Latin America. In the wake of the so-called 15-M Movement (15 May, 2011), the multiple crises (economic, financial, and of political representation), and the realization that urban services were being increasingly privatized, encouraged the implementation of a model based on municipal governance and founded upon this new political grammar.

Our inquiry was developed in the form of questions we asked these newly elected officials from *Barcelona en comù* and their supporters. The challenge of an ethnographic approach within the city hall of Barcelona was taken up based on a protocol we called "Pushing open the doors of city hall,"[1] which progressively unveils the numerous steps involved in

[1] This protocol was utilized within an educational and research project "One Week, One City: Charleroi," with the participation of Laurent Devisme, Pauline Ouvrard, and Elisabeth Pasquier, at the Nantes graduate school of architecture (CRENAU-UMR AAU) in 2015.

the lengthy process that led up to the interview itself. "Pushing open the doors of city hall" means allowing oneself, as an inquirer, to not presume that the political and technical spaces of the city will necessarily be in a distant realm, nor that understanding them will require only objective analysis of political programs and public policies, strategies of action, and networks of stakeholders. It is a descriptive protocol that links analysis and personal narratives in the goal of "playing down" our relationship to political representation. Our inquiry does not seek to take sides or to do justice to some economic, political or "meta-critical" agenda, but rather to understand how knowledge and ideas circulate, through individual trajectories, through ways of doing that have been acquired and transmitted, and through concrete achievements. The challenge of "thinking from the border" was taken up based on a narrative that weaves personal narratives, stories of personal trajectories, the historical skills of those interviewed, and shared reflexivities, and made possible through a series of interviews. Our inquiry straddles the border between intimate citizenship, public citizenship, and the exercise of power, the border between militant action and institutional power, the border between the local and the inter - or transnational scale, as well as the border between memory and history.

Crossing the border between France and Catalonia also led to an encounter and an open, friendly, and serious dialogue between art and the social sciences. The opening up to the field of art called for by our collective research project, enabled us to meet Julia Ramírez Blanco, an art historian and critic, who lives in Barcelona. She proposed a counterpoint or extension in response to Amélie Nicolas's study, based on her analysis of seven artworks which involve political devices for social and urban protests, and artistic utopias. Julia Ramírez Blanco, a specialist in activist practices and utopian visions in contemporary art,[2] proposed a new historiographical source that enabled her to reassess the political situation in Spain, Catalonia, and

[2] Julia Ramírez Blanco, *Artistic Utopias of Revolt: Claremont Road, Reclaim the Streets, and the City of Sol*, (London-New York: Palgrave Macmillan, 2018).

Barcelona in her own way. These seven works of contemporary art accompany and question in other ways the socio-anthropological reading of politics. In this process, the social sciences and art history listen to, share with, and complement each other more than being dissolved in a single heuristic or epistemological ensemble.

"Pushing Open the Doors of City Hall": Investigating the Very Contemporary History of Barcelona

Our inquiry took place over a very short period of time, and at a very particular moment of Spanish history. Indeed, in 2016, no governmental majority could be reached in the general elections, because there was no coalition that supported Mariano Rajoy. Meanwhile, a sharp decline in support for the two political parties that had dominated the scene since the end of the Franco regime (the People's Party (PP) and the Spanish Socialist Workers' Party (PSOE)) was also observed. Finally, two new parties were gaining power, Ciudadanos (a center-right party) and Podemos, which was presented as an alternative left-wing party. This period of political instability gave us the opportunity to recreate a complex history over a relatively short time: since 2011 and the 15-M Movements, and especially, in the context of the rise to power of *Barcelona en Comù*, from January 2014 to May 2015. The memories of those interviewed were very fresh, and they had an obvious desire to transmit them to others. We thus had the chance to conduct these interviews of political staff members who had little concern for political communication, or even better, organized their political communication based on an attitude of empathy and proximity, the guarantee according to them of true political service.[3] "Pushing open the doors of city hall," an "ethnographic" protocol articulated around reflections on the border, is an allusion to the main theme of the interviews requested, to the narratives of a personal, and often militant, history, to that of an

---

[3] Some people also refused to be interviewed because these newly elected officials were overwhelmed with work. Such was the case of Ada Colau, and her three deputy mayors: Girardo Pisarello, Jaume Assens, and Gala Pin, who were away from the city during our inquiry.

institutional history, of political responsibility and partisan commitment. Starting from individual trajectories, sometimes in their intimate or affective dimensions and starting from periodizations and perceptions of watershed events, and from the key moments proposed by those interviewed, we question the possibility of creating a nascent historiographical narrative, and shed light on the tactics of legitimation and action being deployed by those already exercising power.

The 15-M Movements and Partisan Historiography

Our meeting with Steven Forti, an Italian historian of European political cultures, based in Barcelona, and who works as a journalist and correspondent for various Spanish, Catalan, Italian, and Greek periodicals, and is interested in the socio-political analyses of the Spanish, and especially Catalan situation, made it possible to gain a broader vision for writing this very contemporary history. In effect, in February 2016, Steven Forti started writing a book about Ada Colau, with the Italian journalist Giacomo Russo Spena, for the magazine MicroMega.[4] This work was anchored in the context of the municipal elections in Italy. It is a book that had to be written in a very limited amount of time, and he based his approach on a series of interviews in a way that was rather similar to ours. Today, Steven Forti is a member of the *Barcelona en comù* party, and admits that he fully assumes having crossed the border between journalism, which requires a certain critical distance, and partisan historiography, which is linked to his memory of engagement. Having earned his doctoral degree in 2011, Steven Forti told us that he both "observed and participated" in the 15-M Movements in Barcelona. For him, as for some of the other people we interviewed, the 15-M Movements constitute a founding event, which according to Ricoeur, "has the twofold function of breaking with [the past] and creating an origin."[5]

---

[4] Steven Forti and Giacomo Russo Spena. *Ada Colau, La città in comune. Da ocupante di case a sindica di barcellona,* (Rome: Alegre, 2016).

[5] Paul Ricoeur, « Evénement et sens,», a talk given in 1971, and then transcribed and published in «L'espace et le temps,», Proceedings of the 22nd congress of the *Association des sociétés de philosophie de langue française.* (Paris: Vrin, 1991), 9-21. Accessed on:
http://www.fondsricoeur.fr/uploads/medias/articles_pr/evenement-et-sens.pdf, 8. (In French).

For one year, Steven Forti participated in countless mobilizations, which included *mareas sociales,* major thematic events that focus on issues such as healthcare and education. He remembered how at that time it was the leaders of the social movements who organized the political and social debates during this intense period of mobilization. In Barcelona, the action carried out by the Platform for People Affected by Mortgages (PAH) received attention, and was considered to be emblematic of an "alter-activism" that could unite people. At that time, Ada Colau was the spokesperson of this platform, which intended to offer support to families evicted by their landlords (particularly by the banks themselves) because they were unable to make their mortgage payments. Through demonstrations, such as *Caseroladas* (an urban event during which people bang on pots and pans), *Escratchs* (actions that originated in Argentina, and consist in going to the home or workplace of somebody you want to denounce), and *okupas* (occupying housing), the Platform for People Affected by Mortgages developed a methodology based on general assemblies and the dynamics of empowerment, which would ultimately be used as a model for organizing the future *Barcelona en comù* party. The legitimacy acquired via the 15-M experience made it possible to write a new political grammar, and, even more so, a new partisan historiography based on fighting political corruption, denouncing the "revolving doors" pheno-menon (shady relations between politicians and private corporations, lobbies, and institutions), questioning the rigid party-based political system, or in any case its incapacity to adapt to the contemporary world, and developing reflections and resources linked to the commons.

Guanyem Barcelona: Memory and Manifestos

In 2013, there was a decrease in social mobilizations, "the quite logical end of a cycle of mobilization" for Steven Forti. The leaders of the social movements started wondering about the future of the mobilizations, and some tried to "jump into politics." The 15-M

Movements had some influence on the positions of certain social movement representatives, who shifted towards a "we want to win" stance, which resulted in new reflections and a new political language, with the new *Podemos* party taking over the leadership.[6] Steven Forti, shifting from his own personal memories to the writing of this history in Barcelona, told us how meetings were organized around the DESC (Observatory of Economic, Social, and Cultural rights)[7] and "around Ada's circle," which together initiated the *Guanyem Barcelona* (Let's Win back (or Take back) Barcelona) process, with the goal of creating political convergence to be able to put together a list of candidates for the 2015 municipal elections.

We met Joan Subirats at the *Ateneu Barcelonès*, close to Catalunya Square, a former neoclassical palace built in the 18th century, which had been transformed into a cultural center that is used today by Catalan intellectuals. Today he is an economist and a political scientist, who teaches at the Autonomous University of Barcelona, but Joan Subirats was first of all a major figure in the Catalan struggle against Francoism. He would tell us how, in 1973, he was imprisoned for several months, after having been arrested during an anti-Franco assembly, along with one hundred of his comrades. At that time, he was an activist in the "Bandera roja", a left-wing group uniting the Communist Party — in coordination with France —, and a left-wing faction of workers and farmers. At the end of his studies, he became a professor of "political law" at the Autonomous University of Barcelona, a "mixture of constitutional law and political science, which did not exist in Spain at that time." An activist in the Communist Party, he participated in the process during which the Spanish Constitution was discussed. In 1980-1981, he left the Communist Party due to its internal dissensions and would not engage in activist activities again, in the sense of participating

[6] Jeanne Moisand, « Espagne: de l'indignation à l'organisation », *La Vie des idées*, March 20, 2015.
[7] The DESC is a platform created in 1998 that brings together intellectuals and organizations working to defend social rights. Steven Forti presented it to us as a place where "alter-activists" and intellectuals get together, a "kind of 'not in our name,' anti-austerity think tank, of left-wing individuals opposed to the Troika and in favor of people's right to self-determination."

in political party activities, until the citizen-based candidacy of Ada Colau for the 2015 municipal elections. He devised the political manifesto *Guanyem Barcelona*, the guiding thread of the campaign, which was significantly inspired by his 2011 essay grounded in the field of "common studies."[8] On June 26, 2014, the manifesto *Guanyem Barcelona* was officially presented in the El Raval district of Barcelona, and a campaign was launched in the different neighborhoods, in coordination with neighborhood associations.

For this race, *Barcelona en comù* made a clear allusion to a longer historical period, which included the anti-Franco struggle and a questioning of the official historiography of the democratic transition, and the presence of intellectuals and academics, who had been on the left since the anti-Franco combat, was accepted. Behind these names was the history of municipalism in Barcelona and the citizen-activist tradition in its neighborhoods (the *movimiento vecinal*), which was revived, thus confirming the prospects that a neo-municipalism (or *Ciudadanismo*) would be implemented by the new municipal government. The *vecinal* movement was born in the final years of Francoism, in a period of limited political freedom.[9] From 1968 to 1971 it enabled the lower and middle classes to collectively engage in debate and action, as a form of possible resistance to the dictatorship, the only veritable political alternative during a period in which political parties could not be created. The new municipal government has endeavored to reactivate this history of the neighborhoods, particularly in the deliberation process it has put in place for making public policies, and with a firm commitment to neo-municipalism.

The Intimate and the Political

Our interview with Laura Pérez, who had organized and was the Head of a "Gender Transversality" Department, and was developing

---

[8] Joan Subirats, *Otra sociedad, ¿otra política? De "no nos representan" a la democracia de lo común,* (Barcelona: Icaria, 2011).
[9] For more information on municipalism and neighborhood movements, see the research by the Catalan journalist and historian Marc Andreu, who has also joined *Barcelona en comù*.

public policies oriented toward "life cycles, feminisms, and LGBTI", focused especially on the personal trajectory of this activist. From a family in southern Spain that moved to Barcelona, her mother was a housekeeper who worked for wealthy bourgeois Catalan families, and her father was a worker, so they were familiar with life in Barcelona and its outlying predominantly working-class neighborhoods. Having left for South America in 2008, she lived through the 15-M events from Ecuador where she was working for UN Women with indigenous communities from the mountains. In 2012, pregnant with her daughter, she decided to return to Barcelona with her partner. Neither of them had a job. Laura Perez joined *Podemos*, and was a militant in its gender group whose goal was to bring together and unite all of the feminist movements in Barcelona. She was invited to join *Guanyem Barcelona* in the "gender and sexual diversity" group, which was a clear sign of the movement's intention to present a feminist platform and to develop a cross-gender argument on this subject. This is how, once they had won the elections, Laura Perez became the Head of this new Department whose goal is to speak of *feminisms* and of *care* rather than implementing policies that concern early childhood, youth, and old-age by sector (infants, youth, the elderly). Officially adopting and utilizing the term *Feminisms* (in the plural) in this new municipal government, so as to include all feminisms, no longer simply in their theoretical dimensions, but in militant and organizational ones, was at that time a major ideological and political change.

Personal narrative becomes the point of departure for politicizing arguments. It is especially the role of women that marks this institutionalization of the "private life of convictions".[10] She referred to women's conditions in terms of motherhood and political work, in particular, because many women between the age of 30 and 40 have been elected. Their personal narratives and the public expression of their conditions as mothers structure the debates and support "feminist" points of view of

[10] Anne Muxel (ed.), *La vie privée des convictions. Politique, affectivité, intimité*, (Paris: Presses de Sciences Po, 2014).

engaged politics. Speaking about her own condition as a woman politician in office, Laura Perez confided in us about the difficulties linked to her daily schedule. She is the mother of a 3-year old girl, but sees her very little. "We never were people who worked 8 hours and then went home. No, we come from the intense social struggles, with meetings late into the night (…) None of us has had a cushy life (…) three days can go by without seeing your children, your family (…) I don't know if I can keep up with this pace, and I often tell myself that I'll feel lighter in 4 years, I'm trying to find psychological techniques. But I think it's probably worth it." "The personal is political," she reminds us, repeating the feminist slogan of the 1970s. Reactivating this statement has become the point of departure of our program and of the political action to accomplish. These recently elected officials are thus affirming the feminist perspective of their mandates. It is based on the collective and political translation of the intimate condition, henceforth linked to the challenge of a genuine "democracy of the commons," which is first of all, according to Subirats, to assess what affects us personally in our daily lives.

Deglobalization?

Eloi Badia's background lies in the struggles linked to water and energy. He was the spokesperson for the Alliance against energy precarity and an active member of the Catalan platform *Agua es vida*, which campaigns for the deprivatization of water networks. *Agua es vida* is also very closely connected to the PAH (Platform for People Affected by Mortgages), and other similar activist movements whose guiding principle is the need to define basic common resources and denounce the privatization of basic services and rights.[11] Eloi Badia

---

[11] Dominique Lorrain and Gerry Stoker, *La privatisation des services urbains en Europe*, (Paris: La Découverte, 1995). They remind us of the 4 kinds of "privatization" of urban services: 1) the sale of public assets to private companies, 2) the delegation of services via management contracts (concessions, leases, and others), 3) the transformation of public administrations into private stock companies, 4) the introduction of competition into the public sector by adopting private management principles.

was elected because of his position and expertise on water and energy issues and his capacity to manage such contracts for the municipal government. He presented us the demands linked to the commons based on what he believes is a pragmatic observation:

> There has been such a radical degradation of our public services and rights. The crisis and social inequalities, the corruption of our governments. In fact, we have just established a program: a law on mortgages, a condemnation of debt, stop cutting off people's access to energy, the end of corruption, and increased transparency. For us, that's asking for the bare minimum.

He presents his role as a very concrete approach based on knowledge and strategies for redefining power relations or adjusting the public sector to the private sector. He goes on to question the fatalistic discourse on the municipal government's lack of funds and the supposed need to set up speculative urban policies in Barcelona to offset it. Eloi Badia presented us the political and tactical challenges involved in deglobalizing Barcelona, which would require a return to public control of the resources about which the City has long-term expertise, and putting on the political agenda the demands made by social movements and citizen activists.

The question of habitat and tourism is undoubtedly at the heart of a metropolitan paradox in Barcelona. The municipal government has little room for action vis-à-vis tourism. It is based mainly on the municipal team's skills and authority on housing and public space in terms of land use, such as how it can regulate the rental of apartments for the purposes of tourism, with a current moratorium on the licenses granted, including for hotels, and administrative sanctions applied to informal rental "operations" via platforms such as Airbnb. Susanna Segovia, from the executive management of the *Barcelona en comù* party spoke to us about the challenge of "deprivatizing Las Ramblas" in the plan to reform this avenue, by closing the market stalls and refreshment stands and limiting the amount of area rented to cafés and restaurants for their terraces. "Because today, no people from Barcelona sit on these terraces. These are terraces for paella, tapas, sangria, and beer where you have to consume if you want to sit down. There are no longer any public benches—or very few. It has become a hostile place for children." Everyone feels like there has been an "invasion of 'mobile boards'" (kick scooters, Segways, and skateboards), those supposedly low-impact modes of transportation, rented in huge numbers to tourists. The appointment of the artist and activist Agueda Bañon, who is in the "post-porn" movement, as Director of Communication of the City of Barcelona is a move toward reversing the values attached to the touristic attractivity of Barcelona. She analyzes mass tourism there as a form of urban pornography and commodification of bodies, which is linked to the festive ideology attached to the city. Her post-porn perspective, extolling sexual freedoms and feminisms, denounces the mercantile forms of pornography circulating in public space, and builds on the political and feminist perspectives associated with the "detouristification" of the downtown area.

Barcelona, the model city for European metropolitan development, a city that has attracted attention and even been cited and copied for the urban and architectural strategies it has implemented,[12] at least since the 1992 Olympic Games. An international metropolis that has been both culturally and economically successful, a winning city in the development of its advanced tertiary economy, Barcelona has won a spot for itself in the lineup of top European or even worldwide metropolises. *Barcelona en comù's* victory in the municipal elections marks a sharp break with the promotion of this metropolitan model, ultimately making manifest the famous fifth chapter ("Reclaiming the City for Anti-Capitalist Struggle") in David Harvey's latest book.[13] Ada Colau's government undoubtedly

[12] Jordi Borja i Sebastià, *Barcelona: un modelo de transformación urbana, [1980-1995]*, United Nations Urban Development Programme Oficina Regional para América Latina y El Caribe, (Quito, Ecuador: PGU-LAC, 1995). On the other hand, in 2009, he published a retrospective study that was critical of this idea that Barcelona was a model: Jordi Borja i Sebastià, *Luces y sombras del urbanismo de Barcelona*, (Barcelona: Editorial UOC, 2009. From 1983 to 1995, Jordi Borja was the deputy mayor in charge of international relations.

[13] David Harvey, *Rebel Cities: From the Right to the City to the Urban Revolution*, (London, New York: Verso, 2012).

represents what remains invisible in the promotion of the "winning" metropolitan territories, whereas a polarization of urban society is occurring. Deglobalizing Barcelona means to tell the other history that would otherwise be completely overshadowed by the self-fulfilling prophecies of the "winning" metropolis. It means to rewrite the historiography of the city to the benefit of the invisible minorities. As we have seen, it also means promoting other historical characteristics of the city, such as the social revolution of 1936, which was in the minds of all those interviewed; that is, a different foundation than the history of the post-Franco transition. In opposition to globalization, it gives prominence to the history of municipalism in Barcelona and to the associative and political vitality of the neighborhoods.

There is a definite return to local concerns in the *Barcelona en comù* government, which makes us reflect on a possible fascination for the local, as the place for the "natural" development of democracy, especially in Spain, where the forces of determination present at the national level must be put into the context of the history of local autonomies. It makes us reflect on the deglobalization of the city in terms of closing borders, a localism that would ultimately raise fears about international issues. That is often the analytical and critical horizon that can be seen when regionalisms emerge in Europe. For example, in the case of figures such as Pasqual Maragall who wanted to resuscitate the myth of a free Barcelona, Georges Frêche who tried to resuscitate *Septimanie* in France, and Massimo Cacciari who reminded people of the virtues of Venetian forms of government in the age of the Most Serene Republic, thereby reactivating the Medieval myth of the autonomy of urban governments in Europe.[14] "Tourismophobia" would thus be a term, which, according to Manuel Delgado, could lead to "touristophobia" and its negative xenophobic consequences.[15] In this process, points of view become muddled, with demands for Catalan

[14] Patrick Le Galès, *European cities. Social conflict and governance*, (Oxford: Oxford University Press, 2002).
[15] Manuel Delgado, « Turistofobia », *El Pais,* July 12, 2008.

independence, others against capitalism, criticism about a desire to remain isolated and contempt for other places. This question provided food for thought in the discussions we had with our interviewees, and made us attentive to the question of new forms of circulation, beyond the local level—movements of knowledge, people, and episteme within *Barcelona en comù*—, as well as to the emergence of another transnational scene.

Between Here and Elsewhere: The Internationalization of Municipal Government

The professional and activist experiences in Latin America of those we interviewed[16] are particularly interesting in terms of understanding these theoretical and political circulations, and the development, still in its early stages, of new transnational political networks and movements which include Barcelona. All of these circulations result in the construction of scenes for political and social action at various scales, which make it possible to increase the number of spaces for individual and collective engagement, particularly thanks to the social networks. The multiple identities of the members of *Barcelona en comù* (political parties, social movements, and citizen-activist supporters) make it a party that is not very traditional. According to Joan Subirats, "It has a more IKEA identity, more modular. You are here one moment, and elsewhere another. That has to do with Internet and the conception of hackers.

[16] Laura Perez went to South America in 2008, where she worked for UN Women and other organizations on gender-based issues among indigenous communities in the Ecuadorian and Peruvian mountains, and then in Bolivia, El Salvador, and Guatemala. Carlos Marcias, who was at that time studying political science in Barcelona, and is today the PAH spokesperson, travelled in Central America in 2011, where he met different social movement activists, which would subsequently strengthen his commitment to the PAH. Susanna Segovia is on the executive management team of *Barcelona en comù*. She studied journalism, before completing a master's degree in Cooperation and Development, during which she travelled to Ecuador to study the issues of participative democracy and leadership training, notably for *Pachakutic*, the political arm of the indigenous movement. Iolanda Fresnillo is a member of the DESC Observatory, on the basis of her engagement in the citizens network for foreign debt cancellation (based on the Ecuadorian experience), and she supports *Barcelona en comù*. She told us how she joined the drop the debt movements that were gaining importance in Spain in the late 1990s, based on her experience in the movements that campaigned against the debt plaguing southern countries.

You can create a group, and just after divide it, you can move to join forces with others, unite around a project, and then divide up again." The traditional and exclusive militant loyalty to the Party has now been replaced by a belonging to political networks that are at the same time local, regional, national, and transnational. The progressive creation of a network that reaches beyond the local level can already be found in a network of cities won over in Spain to the social movements, citizen-based platforms, and *Podemos*: *Ahora Madrid*, the citizens united platform; *Marea Atlantica* in La Corogne; *Valencia en comù*; *Zaragoza en Común*, *Por Cadiz si se puede*, and others. Beyond these considerations, it is Barcelona's position within a network of refuge-cities that illustrates the internationalization of municipal governments, as well as the meetings bringing together intellectuals, activists, and elected officials based on their opposition to the international, national, and European policies that follow the rules set by the Troika (the European Central Bank, European Commission, and the International Monetary Fund).

It is probably within the pan-European, anti-austerity political movement, Diem25, founded by the philosopher Srecko Horvat, and inspired by Yanis Varoufakis's Manifesto, that *Barcelona en comù* intends to get involved in the sphere of international or at least European action. Ada Colau is one of the founding members of this political movement, and her First Deputy Mayor, Girardo Pisarello, has published a book of dialogues with Yanis Varoufakis,[17] according to whom *"meetings must be held to discuss European democracy in all European cities."* In his speech to launch the Diem 25 movement at the Volksbühne Theater in Berlin on February 9, 2016, Varoufakis declared that "The city council is at the heart of democracy," and that "what Europe needs is a veritable network of the same kind *of* 'rebel cities.'" Tracing back the historical development of urban struggles since the Paris Commune, in his most recent book, David Harvey gives credit to this historiography of urban, anti-capitalist movements demanding human rights. In his genealogy, he sketches out a historical map at the global scale:

---

[17] Yanis Varoufakis and Girardo Pisarello, *Un plan para Europa*, (Barcelona: Icaria, 2016).

Barcelona in 1936, Prague and Paris in 1968, Cordoba in 1969, alterglobalist or antiglobalist gatherings (Seattle in 1999), and concludes by studying the movement of squares (Syntagma, Tahrir, Puerta del Sol) and the protests in Oaxaca and Cochabamba.[18]

In this way, the circulations between the Latin American political experiences, which were transmitted to Europe by a generation of student-militants and young professionals who went there for training, and the organization of a new transnational level of municipal experiences like *Barcelona en comù*, ultimately confirms a "return of European cities" through political action networks working from and in the local territories. *Barcelona en comù* seeks to share its local experience and to take part in a transnational network that is being organized, based on a political grammar that includes issues linked to deglobalization conceived of as a joyful process. Between neo-municipalism and international political alternatives, a new political space has been organized, linking militants and intellectuals engaged in social critique, who, since the case of Barcelona, have shown us they *can* take the power.

CURATING IMAGES. SEVEN PHOTOGRAMS PAVING THE WAY TO AN
ASSAULT ON INSTITUTIONS

In reaction to the results of this inquiry, Julia Ramírez Blanco chose to analyze seven artworks, which taken together or individually, enable us to see and to think about the reasons behind the crisis in Spain with their international implications, and then the protest movements and organizations that tried to respond to them by providing other visions, alternatives, and socio-political projects. Her analysis shows the role played by art as a historiographical "mirror" of the political, and also as a place where new forms and practices of activism and innovative political mechanisms are invented, while revealing the ties between the art world and militant political practices.

[18] David Harvey, *Rebel Cities.*

In particular, she alludes to the general assembly, a mechanism explored by many artists throughout the world over the past decade.

— CLAIRE FONTAINE, *P.I.G.S.*, 2012.

This story begins with the economic crisis caused by the collapse of Lehman Brothers in 2008. PIGS is the acronym that the International Monetary Fund would use in reference to the first countries that experienced a crisis: Portugal, Italy, Greece, and Spain. This term was, however, far from innocuous and it inspired various mobilizations against austerity during which demonstrators wore pig masks.

P.I.G.S. is also the title of a work that the Claire Fontaine collective "restaged" in various contexts (image p.106). It is a map of these southern European countries hanging on a wall, and because it is made of matches appears to be three dimensional. Before it is unveiled to the public, somebody lights this geographic representation with a flamethrower. The videos show how Portugal and Spain, then Italy, and finally Greece burn. Using the flamethrower, the "scorcher" flares up the islands while the fire remains on the continental part as a red contour of incandescent embers. Once the flames have died, a black trace of the dense column of smoke remains on the wall. It is too late when the viewers enter the room. They can only make out the charred remains and see a video of the process, which according to the collective "defines the tragedy of the economic crisis." Linked in its early stages to the Invisible Committee (the author of the famous essay *The Coming Insurrection*), Claire Fontaine and its members allude to the destruction linked to the crisis. Perhaps they also allude to the insurrections, linked to different forms of "austericide," ranging from utopia to confrontations.

— CASSIE THORNTON, *PHYSICAL AUDIT*, 2012.

The economic crisis in southern Europe was closely linked to banking organizations. The North American artist Cassie Thornton incorporates the idea of auditing the debt into her work *Physical Audit* (image p.106). In this project, a group of women enter bank offices and perform a choreography that opposes affective and corporeal elements to the aggressiveness of financial transactions. By touching objects such as ATMs, the women dust the banks, dirt being a sign of human presence. In a series of actions based on trust, they withdraw money collectively from ATMs, while the cardholder is blindfolded. In small groups, they ask the banks to open a collective account. At that moment, they also begin dancing while caressing different objects. These performances took place in different banks, almost every day for a month. These actions remind us of the performances of the activist collective Flo6x8, which also entered banks to perform anti-capitalist Flamenco dances, one of which is called *Es que no hay crisis, se llama capitalismo* (There is no Crisis, Capitalism is its Name).

— MARCO GODOY, *RECLAMAR EL ECO*, 2012.

In Spain, the major reaction in response to the crisis took place through what has become known nationally as the 15-M Movements, because the first erupted on May 15, 2011, when, after a demonstration, a small group of people decided to camp out on Puerta del Sol Square, in Madrid. For almost one month, a complex encampment was set up there, forming a kind of city within the city. Organized according to the model of *okupados* (squatted social centers), a multitude of commissions and work groups held meetings on the Square focusing on pragmatic, political, and cultural issues. Coro 15M was one of these groups.

In his video *Reclamar el eco*, the Spanish artist Marco Godoy brings together a chorus of activists in the conference room of the Law School at the Complutense University of Madrid (image p.106). In this royal hall, the group forms an ensemble that seems to be from another age. It then begins to sing. The slogans shouted in the streets since the beginning of the economic crisis ring out against the Baroque music adapted for the work: "que no nos representan" (you don't represent us), "se va a acabar la paz social" (social peace is coming to an end), "no tenemos miedo" (we are not afraid).

— OLIVER RESSLER, *TAKE THE SQUARE*, 2012.

When Godoy shot his video, the occupation or takeover of public squares had spread, first to all of Spain, and then throughout the world. The video installation by the Austrian artist Oliver Ressler, broadcast on three different channels, focuses on certain aspects of the general assemblies after the encampments in New York, Athens, and Madrid.

Through interviews of militants from the 15-M, Syntagma Square, and Occupy Wall Street movements, Ressler's movie shows us the discussions of work groups that speak directly in front of his camera. Their reflections take up theoretical issues, such as horizontal power and forms of organization, as well as the means for producing social change. As an artist linked to the mobilizations, Ressler affirms that his work "seeks to contribute to improving the organizational knowledge of the movements and to translating the processes between these places in transition."

— PETER SLOTERDIJK, GESA MUELLER VON DER HAEGEN ET DIERK JORDAN, *PNEUMATIC PARLIAMENT*, 2005.

This sense of permanent debate was one of the main characteristics of the different forms of mobilization leading up to the occupation of public squares. The metaphor of democracy as an agora can be expressed through works like *Pneumatic Parliament*, which was designed by Peter Sloterdijk, Gesa Mueller von der Haegen, and Dierk Jordan (image p.106). This object is an inflatable edifice that can be used anywhere in the world to house parliamentary meetings. Its light structure would enable it to be transported easily, and it has a 160-person capacity. According to its description, "the Pneumatic Parliament can provide the architectural conditions required for democratic processes in 24 hours." Even if the project is a bit ironic in the current context, it can be interpreted as a means for pointing out the shortcomings of the democratic system today.

— Las Agencias, vêtements de protection pour les manifestations, série *Prêt à révolter*. 2001.

Not without paradoxes, one of the consequences of this cycle of mobilizations was political institutionalization. In a certain sense, we can also say that institutional experimentation in the field of art preceded its incorporation into politics. One of the first examples in Spain took place in Barcelona, in the framework of the *Las Agencias* project, organized in collaboration with the MACBA (contemporary art museum). In 2000, a group of activists worked with the museum in the goal of creating objects and organizational networks that could mobilize people in the context of the anti-globalization movement. These activists set up the local chapter of Indymedia, made shields and protective clothing, and created signs that would flood the city to prepare for the protests they wanted to organize for the 2001 IMF meeting. Even if the IMF meeting could ultimately not be held in Barcelona, the mobilizations were nonetheless organized in order to use the objects made by *Las Agencias*, which resulted in the police actually charging on the demonstrators in the museum. Although it ended in conflict, this experience was perhaps one of the first occasions that enabled activism to imagine a way of incorporating its goals and ways of taking action into the context of a public institution. Ada Colau, the future mayor of Barcelona for the *Barcelona en comù party*, was one of the members of *Las Agencias*.

— Shaun Slifer, collectif Just Seeds, *Teach History from Below*, 2015.

In this process of politicizing and reflecting on activist practices in themselves, most of the studies and other documents were prepared by the participants themselves. In this setting, the idea of activist research emerged, because the different voices could not hide the fact that they were part of the history they were telling. As an imperative, Shaun Slifer, who was in the art collective Just Seeds, exhorted participants to: "Teach history from below."

DECENTERING

The encounter and dialogue, initiated through the processes involved in conducting and writing an inquiry, between a sociologist and an art historian, will have enabled us to experience the decentering involved in any new research approach. This decentering was made possible by the different phases of the inquiry, and by the playful processes of listening, transcription, and translation. It is a decentering also produced through the eyes of art.

Our meeting constitutes a fundamental questioning of history, of how it is written and reconstructed, its ways of approaching events, its corpuses and biases, as well as how it is publicized. Choosing to reconstruct the "institutional leap" made by activists who were elected to office, based on an inquiry that gave preference to personal accounts, made the sociologist in this study reflect on the role she chose to take on—as a public letter-writer, journalist, or official historiographer of the new party? In this history, the field of art occupies a position that is definitely not external. Julia Ramírez Blanco writes about certain activist processes invented in art world institutions, such as the *Las Agencias* initiative at the MACBA, where important figures, closely linked to the new political party *Barcelona en comù,* can be found bustling around and preparing themselves for action. Art, of course, raises questions and makes commentaries, but when friendship also comes into play, it can provide specific tools needed to express the concerns of these political and social movements and the issues they address. From this point of view, the field of art does not neglect to work on history from the overlapping perspectives of the intimate and the political, and political commitment based on affect. After having engaged in this interdisciplinary dialogue, reflecting on the place of friendship, at the border of the intimate and the political and of the arts and the human and social sciences, would require us to reflect back on the origins of a political group founded upon a friendly relationship and the same engagement in social movements. "Friends," "camarades," "brothers," and "*compañeros*": all of these words elicit reflections on forms of political associations, which, according to the contexts, are publicly acclaimed, alluded to, or instead concealed and discredited. Reflecting on friendship, means in this context rethinking "philia" as the first step in forming a political group as Aristotle presents it in *Book 8* of *Nicomachean Ethics,*[19] or to consider it, on the contrary, as something suspicious or even deviant, because it would be, for example, an opaque and illegitimate element undermining republican equality. Whereas the human and social sciences have to a large extent failed to account for the role of friendship, either because it does not seem to be an apprehendable social phenomenon, or because it is considered to constitute a bias, we could envision the places and practices of the arts as the means that can grasp and recreate the immanent organization of political action entailed by friendship.

* Julia Ramírez Blanco co-wrote this article with Amélie Nicolas, and is an art historian and critic. She is currently completing post-doctoral research on a Juan de la Cierva grant while teaching in the Art History Department at the University of Barcelona. Her most recent and internationally acclaimed work *Utopías Artísticas de revuelta* explores the relationships between art, utopia, and social change. It was published in English in 2018 as *Artistic Utopias of Revolt* (London, New York: Palgrave-MacMillan). Her articles have been published in English, French, Italian, and Spanish, in various collective works, and in reviews and journals such as Third Text. Julia Ramírez Blanco collaborates regularly with different institutions, including the MACBA in Barcelona.

[19] Aristotle, *Nicomachean Ethics, Books VIII and IX*, trans. Michael Pakuluk (Oxford, New York: Oxford University Press, 1998).

Printed by

PETRO OFSETAS

Lithuania

EUROPE

August 2019